Blood in the Heartland:

Notorious Wisconsin Murderers

Scott Bowser

© 2024 by Scott Bowser

All rights reserved. No part of this book may be reproduced, stored in a retrieval system or transmitted in any form or by any form or by any means without prior written permission by the author.

TABLE OF CONTENTS

Forward..7

Chapter 1

    Ed Gein..9

Chapter 2

    James McBriar..19

Chapter 3

    David Spanbauer...28

Chapter 4

    Jeffrey Dahmer..41

Chapter 5

    Walter Ellis...54

Chapter 6

    Steven Zelich...64

Chapter 7

    Ashlee Martinson..70

Chapter 8

    Steven Avery……………………...……76

Chapter 9

    Joseph Franklin……………………...…86

Chapter 10

    Gerald Turner………………………….96

Chapter 11

    Chai Vang…………………………….105

Chapter 12

    Radcliff Haughton…………..………....112

Chapter 13

    Laurie Bembenek……………..……….119

Chapter 14

    Edward Edwards……………………...128

Chapter 15

    Richard Otto Macek……………………134

Chapter 16

    Tyler Peterson………………………………...141

Chapter 17

    Christopher Scarver……………….……..149

Chapter 18

    Jon McGaffary………………………………..156

Chapter 19

    Terry Ratzmann………………….………..163

Chapter 20

    Jesse Anderson……………………………172

Final Thoughts………………………………..181

FORWARD

Wisconsin, often known for its picturesque landscapes and Midwestern charm, hides a darker side beneath its serene surface. The state is home to some of the most chilling and notorious murders in American history. In this book, we will delve into the macabre world of Wisconsin murders, exploring cases that have shocked communities, confounded investigators, and left a permanent mark on the state's collective memory. Through a meticulous examination of these crimes, we aim to understand the motivations behind them, the investigative challenges they presented, and the lasting impact they had on the victims' families and society at large.

Wisconsin's history is punctuated by a series of chilling and often perplexing murders. From the grotesque crimes of Ed Gein and Jeffrey Dahmer to the controversial conviction of Steven Avery, each case presents its own set of questions and challenges. By examining these stories, we aim to shed light on the darker aspects of human nature and the continuous efforts of law enforcement and society to seek justice. This book serves not only as a chronicle of Wisconsin's most infamous murders but also as a reflection on the complexities of crime and the enduring quest for truth.

Chapter 1

Ed Gein

Ed Gein: The Butcher of Plainfield

Ed Gein, often referred to as the "Butcher of Plainfield," is one of America's most infamous criminals. His grotesque crimes, discovered in the late 1950s, shocked the nation and have since inspired numerous books, movies, and television shows. Gein's life and actions provide a chilling glimpse into the mind of a man whose deeds were as bizarre as they were horrifying.

Early Life

Edward Theodore Gein was born on August 27, 1906, in La Crosse County, Wisconsin, to George and Augusta Gein. His upbringing was far from typical. Augusta was a fanatically religious woman who held an intense disdain for her husband and all other men. She believed that all women (except herself) were instruments of the devil and preached these beliefs to her sons, Edward and his older brother, Henry. George Gein, an alcoholic, was largely passive, leaving Augusta to dominate the household.

The family moved to a farm in Plainfield, Wisconsin, in the early 1910s. Isolated from the rest of the community, Augusta further controlled her sons' lives, forbidding them from making friends or having any contact with outsiders. She often read to them from the Bible, selecting passages that reinforced her views on the inherent immorality of the world. This oppressive environment had a profound effect on Ed, shaping his psyche in ways that would later manifest in his horrific crimes.

Tragic Losses

Ed's childhood was marked by significant losses. His father, George, died of heart failure due to his alcoholism in 1940. In 1944, Ed's brother Henry died under mysterious circumstances. Although the official cause of death was asphyxiation from smoke while fighting a brush fire, many suspect that Ed was involved in his brother's demise. Henry had begun to criticize Augusta, which likely did not sit well with Ed.

The most significant loss for Ed came in 1945 when Augusta suffered a series of strokes and died. Her death left Ed devastated. He was utterly dependent on his mother, both emotionally and practically. With her gone, Ed was alone on the family farm, left to his own devices and dark fantasies.

Descent into Madness

After Augusta's death, Ed became increasingly reclusive. He maintained the farm, but it gradually fell into disrepair. Ed's isolation and the deep psychological scars left by his mother's influence began to manifest in bizarre and disturbing behavior. He became obsessed with reading books about Nazi atrocities, medical experiments, and human anatomy. He also developed an interest in adventure stories and pornography.

Ed's twisted interests led him to begin grave robbing. Between 1947 and 1952, he exhumed numerous bodies from local cemeteries. He later confessed to making about 40 nocturnal visits to three local graveyards to exhume recently buried bodies. He would take the corpses home, where he used the skin and bones to create macabre trophies and household items. These gruesome artifacts included chairs upholstered in human skin, skull bowls, and a lampshade made from a human face.

The Crimes Uncovered

Ed's activities might have remained undiscovered if not for his murder of two women. On December 8, 1954, Plainfield tavern owner Mary Hogan disappeared. Her last known whereabouts were at her tavern, which was found in disarray with blood stains on the floor. It wasn't until three years later, however, that the truth about her fate would be revealed.

On November 16, 1957, Bernice Worden, a local hardware store owner, vanished. Her son, Deputy Sheriff Frank Worden, reported her missing after finding the store's cash register open and blood stains leading out the back. Investigating her disappearance, the police soon focused on Ed Gein, who had been seen at the store the evening before.

When police arrived at the Gein farm, they were unprepared for the horrors that awaited them. In a shed, they discovered the decapitated body of Bernice Worden, hung upside down and gutted like a deer. Inside the house, officers found a scene that would haunt them forever: human skulls mounted on bedposts, a collection of human noses, a belt made from human nipples, and a suit made entirely of human skin, among other gruesome artifacts. Mary Hogan's face was also found, along with other body parts from at least 15 women.

Arrest and Trial

Ed Gein was arrested and charged with the murders of Bernice Worden and Mary Hogan. He quickly confessed to killing Worden and Hogan, but his defense argued that he was insane. A team of doctors examined Gein and determined that he was mentally unfit to stand trial. He was sent to the Central State Hospital for the Criminally Insane (later the Mendota Mental Health Institute) in Madison, Wisconsin.

In 1968, after spending more than a decade in mental institutions, Gein was deemed competent to stand trial. The trial, held in Waushara County Court, lasted only one week. Gein was found guilty of the murder of Bernice Worden but was also declared legally insane. As a result, he was committed to a mental hospital for the rest of his life.

Psychological Profile

Understanding what drove Ed Gein to commit such horrific acts has fascinated psychologists and criminologists for decades. Gein's behavior is often analyzed through the lens of his complex relationship with his mother. Augusta's domineering and puritanical influence profoundly shaped Ed's worldview, instilling in him a deep fear and hatred of women, along with a pathological need to possess and control them.

Gein's grave robbing and creation of human trophies can be seen as attempts to recreate his mother and keep her close. The "woman suit" he crafted from human skin is particularly telling; it suggests that Gein was trying to literally step into his mother's role, merging his identity with hers. This act of creating and wearing a suit made from female skin points to extreme psychosexual issues, including possible gender dysphoria, though such diagnoses were not well understood or applied at the time.

Gein's case also illustrates the impact of severe isolation and a lack of social support. After his mother's death, Gein had no significant relationships or community ties, allowing his dark fantasies to flourish unchecked. His isolation, combined with his fascination with death and the macabre, created a perfect storm for the development of his violent tendencies.

Cultural Impact

The discovery of Ed Gein's crimes had a profound impact on American culture and the horror genre. Gein's gruesome deeds inspired numerous fictional characters and stories, most notably Norman Bates in Alfred Hitchcock's "Psycho," Leatherface in "The Texas Chainsaw Massacre," and Buffalo Bill in "Silence of the Lambs." These characters, like Gein, are portrayed as deeply disturbed individuals whose horrific actions stem from complex psychological issues.

Gein's case also influenced the way society views serial killers and the mentally ill. His story highlighted the need for better mental health care and more effective monitoring of individuals with known psychological issues. It also underscored the potential dangers of extreme isolation and the importance of community and social support in preventing such tragedies.

The Farm and Its Aftermath

The Gein farm, where so many horrors were discovered, was burned to the ground in 1958, under mysterious circumstances. Some speculate that it was an act of arson committed by residents who wanted to erase the stain of Gein's crimes from their community. Others believe it was an accidental fire. Regardless, the destruction of the farm marked the end of a dark chapter in Plainfield's history.

Ed Gein remained in mental institutions until his death on July 26, 1984, at the age of 77. He spent the last years of his life at the Mendota Mental Health Institute, where he was reportedly a model patient. Despite the notoriety of his crimes, Gein remained largely unrepentant and detached from the horror he had inflicted.

Legacy

Ed Gein's legacy is a complex one. On one hand, he is remembered as one of the most grotesque and depraved criminals in American history. His crimes continue to fascinate and horrify people, serving as a reminder of the darkest aspects of human nature. On the other hand, Gein's story has contributed significantly to our understanding of criminal psychology and the factors that can drive a person to commit such heinous acts.

Gein's case also sparked important discussions about mental health, the treatment of the criminally insane, and the importance of early intervention and support for individuals with psychological issues. His life and crimes have been the subject of countless books, movies, and documentaries, each attempting to unravel the mystery of what led Ed Gein down his dark path.

Conclusion

Ed Gein's story is one of tragedy, horror, and a deep psychological disturbance. From his troubled upbringing and oppressive relationship with his mother to his descent into madness and the gruesome acts he committed, Gein's life offers a chilling glimpse into the mind of a man whose actions defy comprehension. His legacy serves as a stark reminder of the potential for darkness that exists within the human soul and the importance of understanding and addressing the psychological factors that can lead to such extreme behavior. Through studying cases like Gein's, we hope to gain insights that can help prevent similar tragedies in the future and provide support for those who may be on a path toward such darkness.

Ed Gein

Chapter 2

James McBrair

The Tragic Events of Sunday Morning: A Detailed Account of the James McBrair Jr. Case

Introduction

In a tragic turn of events that shocked the community, James McBrair Jr. has been charged with the first-degree murders of his estranged wife, her stepfather, her stepsister, and a babysitter. This harrowing incident unfolded early on a Sunday morning and has left a community grappling with grief and disbelief. This detailed account seeks to unravel the circumstances leading up to and following these tragic events, providing a comprehensive understanding of this deeply distressing case.

Background of James McBrair Jr.

James McBrair Jr., a resident of Plainfield, Wisconsin, was known in the community as a quiet and reserved individual. Born into a well-regarded family, James was perceived as a dedicated worker and a devoted family man. However, beneath the surface, there were signs of personal struggles and emotional turmoil that would ultimately culminate in this horrific crime.

James and his estranged wife, Emily McBrair, had been facing marital difficulties for several years. Their relationship had deteriorated to the point where they had separated, and Emily was living with her family. James's mental state had become increasingly unstable, with reports of erratic behavior and deepening resentment toward Emily and her family. Despite efforts by friends and family to offer support, James's struggles seemed to spiral out of control.

The Day of the Tragedy

On that fateful Sunday morning, the peaceful quiet of Plainfield was shattered by an unimaginable act of violence. It was around 4:00 AM when James McBrair Jr. reportedly arrived at the home of Emily McBrair, where she lived with her stepfather, Tom Hargrove, her stepsister, Sarah Hargrove, and a babysitter named Jessica Miller, who was there to care for the children.

James had been experiencing significant emotional distress, and his actions on this day reflected a profound sense of rage and desperation. He had managed to obtain a key to the Hargrove residence, which allowed him to gain access to the home unannounced. This crucial detail highlights the premeditation and planning involved in the tragic events that unfolded.

The Murders

James's arrival at the Hargrove home was marked by violence and chaos. According to investigators, James had armed himself with a knife and a blunt object, which he used to commit the murders. The sequence of events, as pieced together from forensic evidence and witness testimonies, is both disturbing and heart-wrenching.

Emily McBrair was the first victim, found in her bedroom with multiple stab wounds. Her stepfather, Tom Hargrove, was discovered in the living room, also suffering from fatal stab wounds and blunt force trauma. Sarah Hargrove, the stepsister, was found in the kitchen, having been attacked with the same brutality. The babysitter, Jessica Miller, who had been sleeping on the couch, was the final victim, killed in a senseless act of violence.

The brutality of the attacks was evident, with each victim having sustained significant injuries. The crime scene was described as chaotic, with evidence of a violent struggle and the presence of blood throughout the house. The severity of the violence underscored the intensity of James McBrair Jr.'s rage and emotional instability.

The Investigation

The investigation into the murders began almost immediately after the police received a call from a concerned neighbor who had heard disturbing noises coming from the Hargrove residence. When officers arrived at the scene, they were met with the horrifying reality of the crime, and the initial focus was on securing the scene and providing aid to any survivors.

Detectives quickly identified James McBrair Jr. as the prime suspect. His estranged wife and her family had been involved in a contentious legal battle with him over custody of their children and division of property. This ongoing conflict provided a motive for the murders, though it did not fully explain the extent of the violence.

James was apprehended a few hours after the murders, found driving erratically in a nearby town. He was taken into custody without incident and was later charged with four counts of first-degree murder. The arrest marked the beginning of a lengthy legal process that would seek to bring justice for the victims and closure to the grieving community.

The Legal Proceedings

James McBrair Jr.'s legal battle began with his arraignment, where he faced multiple charges related to the murders. The courtroom was filled with the victims' family members, friends, and community members seeking answers and justice. The prosecution presented a compelling case, detailing the evidence against James, including forensic evidence, witness statements, and James's own statements made during the investigation.

The defense, on the other hand, sought to present a case of diminished capacity, arguing that James's mental state at the time of the murders had been severely compromised. They cited his history of emotional and psychological issues, including previous reports of depression and instability. The defense's strategy was to argue that James was not fully in control of his actions and that his capacity to understand the consequences of his behavior was impaired.

The trial was intense and emotional, with heartbreaking testimonies from the victims' family members. The prosecution's case was bolstered by the forensic evidence, including DNA samples, fingerprints, and the details of the crime scene. The defense's arguments were scrutinized, and the question of James's mental state became a central point of contention.

The Verdict and Sentencing

After a lengthy trial, the jury found James McBrair Jr. guilty of all charges. The verdict was met with a mixture of relief and sorrow, as the community grappled with the finality of the decision and the enduring pain of the loss. The sentencing phase of the trial followed, during which the judge heard statements from the victims' family members and reviewed the details of James's mental health history.

James was sentenced to life in prison without the possibility of parole. The sentence was intended to reflect the gravity of the crimes and the need to ensure that James would never inflict further harm. The court's decision was a significant step toward justice for the victims and their families, though it did little to alleviate the deep-seated grief and trauma experienced by the community.

Community Impact and Reflection

The murders of Emily McBrair, Tom Hargrove, Sarah Hargrove, and Jessica Miller left an indelible mark on the Plainfield community. The town, known for its close-knit and supportive atmosphere, was shaken by violence and loss. Community members came together to support one another, participating in vigils and memorial services to honor the victims and offer condolences to their families.

The tragedy prompted a broader conversation about mental health, domestic violence, and the challenges faced by families experiencing emotional and psychological distress. It also highlighted the importance of community support systems and the need for early intervention in addressing mental health issues.

In the years following the murders, the community continued to mourn the loss and work toward healing. The victims were remembered with love and respect, and their families found solace in the support of friends, neighbors, and fellow community members. The legacy of their lives and the tragedy of their deaths became a poignant reminder of the need for compassion and vigilance in addressing the complexities of mental health and family dynamics.

Conclusion

The story of James McBrair Jr. and the murders of his estranged wife, her stepfather, her stepsister, and a babysitter are a deeply tragic and complex narrative. It underscores the devastating impact of unresolved emotional turmoil and the far-reaching consequences of violence within a community. As

Plainfield continues to reflect on these events, the memories of the victims serve as a powerful reminder of the importance of understanding, support, and empathy in the face of adversity.

The case of James McBrair Jr. remains a sobering chapter in the history of Plainfield, Wisconsin—a chapter marked by profound loss, intense legal battles, and the enduring quest for justice. The community's resilience and dedication to honoring the victims offer a measure of hope and a commitment to ensuring that such a tragedy is never forgotten.

James McBrair in cuffs

Chapter 3

David Spanbauer

The Chilling Saga of David Spanbauer: A Detailed Account of a Wisconsin Serial Killer

David Spanbauer, a name synonymous with horror and brutality, is one of Wisconsin's most notorious serial killers. His heinous acts of violence, targeting vulnerable women, shocked the community and left a dark legacy in the state's criminal history. This comprehensive account delves into Spanbauer's background, his crimes, the investigation, and the profound impact on the community.

Early Life and Background

David Spanbauer was born in Wisconsin, a state known for its serene landscapes and close-knit communities. However, Spanbauer's upbringing was far from idyllic. Born in the late 1960s, Spanbauer's early life was marked by instability and hardship. His family struggled with financial difficulties, and his parents' tumultuous relationship added to the chaos of his formative years.

Spanbauer's childhood was characterized by frequent moves and a lack of stability, which contributed to his emotional and psychological issues. He had a troubled academic record and struggled to form healthy relationships. His interactions with peers were often fraught with conflict, and he exhibited behavioral problems that went largely unchecked.

As he grew older, Spanbauer's mental health issues became more pronounced. He experienced periods of depression and anxiety but received little to no professional help. His inability to cope with these challenges, combined with his strained family dynamics, set the stage for his eventual descent into violent behavior.

The Path to Violence

Spanbauer's transition from troubled youth to a violent offender was gradual but marked by significant warning signs. His early adulthood was marred by failed relationships and periods of unemployment. He exhibited erratic behavior and struggled with substance abuse, further exacerbating his mental health issues.

Despite several run-ins with the law, Spanbauer's criminal history prior to his murders was relatively minor. He had been arrested for various offenses, including petty theft and assault, but these incidents did not fully reveal the depth of his underlying issues. His pattern of escalating violence, however, suggested a troubling trajectory that would eventually culminate in his gruesome crimes.

Spanbauer's psychological profile revealed a complex mix of traits that contributed to his violent tendencies. He displayed symptoms of antisocial personality disorder, characterized by a lack of empathy and a disregard for the rights of others. His behavior suggested a deep-seated anger and a need for control, which ultimately manifested in his violent acts.

The Murders

David Spanbauer's reign of terror began in the early 1990s and was marked by a series of brutal murders that shocked the community. His victims were all women, chosen seemingly at random but targeted for their vulnerability. The following sections detail the murders of Laura Depies, Ronelle Eichstedt, and Cora Jones, which constitute some of the most heinous crimes attributed to Spanbauer.

Laurie Depies

Investigation Discovery's 'Still a Mystery: The Stuff of Nightmares' depicts how 20-year-old Laurie Depies disappeared under mysterious circumstances in Menasha, Wisconsin, in August 1992. With more than three decades since the incident, has she returned home safely? Also, given several shocking developments, have the police found any conclusive proof of what happened to Laurie? If you want to learn more about this case, here's what we know.

What Happened to Laurie Depies?

Laurie Jean Depies was born to Mark Depies and Mary Mollen Wegner in Wisconsin on September 17, 1971. Her father remembered her endearing qualities, including her easygoing nature and sense of adventure. Mark said, "She was spontaneous. That was Laurie." Friends say Laurie was fun to be around, enjoyed working with people, and was strong-willed. Hence, it was a shock when the 20-year-old disappeared under mysterious circumstances in August 1992.

Laurie Depies

According to reports, Laurie worked at the Graffiti store at Fox River Mall in Grand Chute,

Menasha, and reported for work in the early afternoon of August 19. She was last seen leaving the mall at approximately 10:00 PM that day. She has not been seen since. Police sources stated Laurie arrived at her boyfriend's apartment complex in the 300 block of West Wilson Avenue in Menasha between 10:15 PM and 10:30 PM after leaving work.

Laurie's boyfriend had been waiting for her in his apartment with his sister and a friend. They claimed to have heard her car pull into the parking lot. However, when Laurie did not arrive after a few minutes, the group went looking for her when she did not enter the apartment. After not finding her in the parking lot, her boyfriend informed the police at around 11:45 PM. The authorities interviewed witnesses to learn Laurie was last seen entering her gray 1984 Volkswagen Bug or Volkswagen Rabbit at the Fox River Mall in Grand Chute. The officers found her locked vehicle in the complex parking lot.

In addition, the investigators discovered a Styrofoam cup of soda on the hood of Laurie's car. Yet, there were no other signs of her at the scene. The 20-year-old's overnight bag and purse were also left in the vehicle. Besides, no one saw her walk away from the parking lot or enter anyone's car. Authorities believed Laurie was taken by someone she knew since it was uncharacteristic of her to go with a stranger. Moreover, they found no indication she was forcibly kidnapped. It further strengthened their hypothesis that the young woman left with someone she knew and was possibly harmed later.

Laurie Depies Still Remains Missing

Sadly, Laurie Depies remains missing as of writing, and the investigation into her disappearance continues. The authorities had most of Laurie's friends, including her boyfriend, take polygraph tests. Nevertheless, they were soon cleared of suspicion, and the authorities tried to sort out all other possible angles, leads, and suspects. They found no witnesses seeing Laurie Walk away from the parking lot or get into anyone else's car. According to police sources, the detectives found an unidentified thumbprint on the cup on the hood of her car. They believed it may have been from the alleged abduction suspect, and the size of the print indicated it might have been a man.

According to reports, Laurie picked up a ring she bought for her boyfriend from the mall jewelry store at 7:00 PM. She closed the Graffiti store where she worked around 9:00 PM and walked with her co-worker to the mall parking lot at 9:50 PM. The police interviewed witnesses and checked surveillance footage to find the 20-year-old's last known sighting at 10:00 PM as she drove east on College Avenue and her colleague drove south on US 41. When the authorities exhausted all leads, the case went cold for nearly two decades.

Things suddenly turned when a convict named Larry DeWayne Hall **confessed** to kidnapping and killing Laurie in 2010. He was serving a life sentence for another kidnapping and murder at the time. Larry was considered a suspect in Laurie's case in 1995, along with other murders. The authorities searched the area where he stated he buried her body but found nothing. No physical evidence substantiated Larry's confession, and law enforcement officials eventually discarded his statements.

No arrests have been made for Laurie's disappearance, and her case remains unsolved. Besides, the police have found no activity on her bank accounts or Social Security Number since she went missing. Laurie's father, Mark Depies, stated, "I've accepted that she's dead. But the fact remains, what happened?" On the other hand, her mother, Mary Mollen Wegner, said, "I would just like to know what happened and why it happened just to know that she's at peace."

Mary added, "Because you can't even, you know, have a funeral, or a memorial, or anything, because there's nothing other than her car and a coffee cup, or a soda cup and no story just, you know, off the face of the earth." According to police sources, she has brown hair and green eyes. Her ears have three piercings, and she has a tribal art form tattoo that looks like a squid on the outside of her right ankle

Ronelle Eichstedt

On August 23, 1992, ten-year-old Ronelle Eichstedt went missing. Her bicycle was found near her rural home in Ripon in Fond du Lac County. Her body was found six weeks later a few miles away from her home. Ronelle's body was found in a cornfield ditch near Tower Hill State Park, close to the Wisconsin River.

Cora Jones

On Labor Day, September 5th, a 12-year-old Cora Jones was riding her bike on Sanders Road near her grandma's house in Daytown township. He got Cora into his car and molested her. He drove 75 miles north up to Langlade County near Kempster. Five or six hours later he finally decided to end it. He strangled and stabbed her and threw her body into a steep ditch. Police organized a search for the missing girl and hundreds of volunteers helped canvass the surrounding woods in a ten-mile perimeter. The FBI also joined the case. Her body was found body five days later.

Arrest and Investigation

The investigation into David Spanbauer's activities began with the disappearance of his victims and the subsequent discovery of their bodies. Law enforcement officials focused on Spanbauer due to evidence linking him to the crime scenes and his known criminal history.

Spanbauer was arrested in 1992 after a thorough investigation. His arrest was based on a combination of forensic evidence, witness testimonies, and his own confessions. The evidence collected during the investigation included DNA, fingerprints, and other forensic data that linked Spanbauer to the murders.

Trial and Conviction

David Spanbauer's trial was a highly publicized event. The prosecution presented a strong case based on the forensic evidence and testimonies from survivors and witnesses. The emotional impact of the trial was heightened by the presence of the victims' families and the graphic nature of the evidence presented.

The defense argued that Spanbauer's mental health issues played a significant role in his criminal behavior. Expert witnesses testified about his psychological state, attempting to provide context for his actions. However, the prosecution's case was compelling, and Spanbauer's guilt was evident from the evidence and his own admissions.

In 1993, David Spanbauer was convicted of multiple counts of murder. He was sentenced to life in prison without the possibility of parole. The severity of his crimes and the evidence presented during the trial led to a harsh sentence that reflected the gravity of his actions.

Impact and Legacy

David Spanbauer's crimes had a profound impact on the communities affected by his actions. The families of his victims endured immense suffering and grief as they dealt with the loss of their loved ones. The terror and violence inflicted by Spanbauer left lasting scars on those who were directly impacted by his crimes.

The case also brought attention to issues related to mental health and violence. Spanbauer's background and psychological state were significant factors in the discussions surrounding his crimes. The case highlighted the need for early intervention and support for individuals with mental health issues to prevent similar tragedies.

Spanbauer's legacy is a grim reminder of the capacity for violence within individuals and the importance of addressing underlying psychological and social issues. His actions serve as a case study in criminal behavior, forensic investigation, and the legal system's response to serial killers.

Conclusion

David Spanbauer remains a notorious figure in the history of Wisconsin's criminal landscape. His series of murders, characterized by brutality and violence, left a lasting impact on the victims, their families, and the communities affected by his actions. The investigation, trial, and subsequent imprisonment of Spanbauer reflect the efforts of law enforcement and the legal system to address and respond to severe criminal behavior.

His case serves as a somber reminder of the complexities of criminal psychology and the need for vigilance and support in preventing and addressing violence. The story of David Spanbauer reflects both the darkness that can exist within individuals and the resilience of those who work to bring justice and healing to affected communities.

David Spanbauer

Chapter 4

Jeffrey Dahmer

Jeffrey Dahmer: The Milwaukee Cannibal

Jeffrey Lionel Dahmer, known infamously as the "Milwaukee Cannibal," is one of the most notorious serial killers in American history. His horrific crimes, involving murder, dismemberment, and cannibalism, shocked the nation and left a lasting impact on how society and the criminal justice system address such extreme cases of criminal behavior. This comprehensive examination of Dahmer's life, crimes, and the aftermath of his actions provides insight into one of the darkest chapters in criminal history.

Early Life and Background

Jeffrey Dahmer was born on May 21, 1960, in Milwaukee, Wisconsin, to Lionel and Joyce Dahmer. His early childhood appeared relatively normal, though his family life was far from perfect. Lionel Dahmer was a research chemist, while Joyce Dahmer was a teletype machine instructor. Their marriage was troubled, marked by frequent arguments and emotional distance. This instability in the household likely contributed to Jeffrey's psychological development.

From a young age, Dahmer exhibited disturbing behavior. As early as four years old, he displayed an unusual fascination with dead animals. He collected roadkill and dissected it, an interest that would later evolve into his violent criminal acts. During his formative years, Dahmer was socially isolated and struggled with alcoholism. His academic performance declined, and he often acted out in destructive ways, such as setting fires or engaging in petty theft.

Dahmer's behavior became increasingly erratic as he entered adolescence. He was described as a loner with few friends and a growing tendency toward alcohol abuse. This self-destructive behavior alienated him from his peers and contributed to his eventual expulsion from high school. Despite his apparent intelligence, Dahmer's academic and social difficulties foreshadowed the troubles that would follow.

The First Kill

In June 1978, shortly after his high school graduation, Dahmer committed his first murder. He lured a 19-year-old neighbor, Steven Hicks, to his home with promises of alcohol. Once there, Dahmer bludgeoned Hicks to death with a dumbbell, then dismembered his body and disposed of the remains. This murder marked the beginning of a gruesome spree that would last over a decade.

Dahmer's early crimes were characterized by a disturbing pattern. After killing his victims, he would engage in acts of necrophilia, cannibalism, and dismemberment. He preserved body parts, including skulls and genitalia, which he kept as trophies. This behavior was part of Dahmer's desire to create "zombies" — individuals whom he believed he could control entirely.

The Pattern of Violence

Over the next 13 years, Dahmer's killing spree continued. His crimes followed a disturbing and recognizable pattern:

1. **Victim Selection**: Dahmer targeted young men, often from marginalized communities. Many of his victims were people of color or individuals struggling with addiction. He used deception to lure his victims, offering money, alcohol, or companionship.
2. **Murder and Dissection**: Once his victims were in Dahmer's apartment, he would drug them to render them unconscious before strangling them to death. After killing them, Dahmer would dismember their bodies, often keeping parts for later use.
3. **Cannibalism and Necrophilia**: Dahmer admitted to eating parts of his victims and engaging in sexual acts with their remains. These acts were driven by a desire for power and control over his victims, as well as a fascination with the human body.

4. **Preservation of Body Parts**: Dahmer collected and preserved various body parts from his victims. He displayed some of these remains in his apartment and kept others in his refrigerator or freezer. This macabre collection was a testament to his obsession with death and control.

VICTIMS:

Jeffrey Dahmer, one of the most notorious serial killers in American history, was responsible for the murders of 17 young men and boys between 1978 and 1991. His victims came from various backgrounds and were targeted for their vulnerability. Here is a list of Dahmer's known victims:

1. **Steven Hicks** (June 18, 1978): A high school classmate of Dahmer's, Hicks was 19 years old when Dahmer lured him to his home with the promise of alcohol. Dahmer bludgeoned Hicks to death with a dumbbell, then dismembered and disposed of his body.
2. **Steven Tuomi** (November 20, 1987): Dahmer picked up 24-year-old Tuomi at a bar. Dahmer drugged and strangled him, then dismembered his body and disposed of the remains. Tuomi was one of Dahmer's first

victims after his release from his first stint in prison.
3. **James Doxtator** (January 1988): A 14-year-old boy, Doxtator was lured to Dahmer's apartment. Dahmer drugged him, killed him, and dismembered his body.
4. **Richard Guerrero** (March 24, 1988): Guerrero, 22, was another victim whom Dahmer lured to his apartment. He was drugged, killed, and dismembered.
5. **Anthony Sears** (March 25, 1989): Sears, 26, was an aspiring model. Dahmer lured him to his apartment, drugged, killed, and dismembered him, keeping some of his body parts as trophies.
6. **Eddie Smith** (May 31, 1990): Dahmer lured Smith, a 27-year-old male prostitute, to his apartment. After drugging, killing, and dismembering him, Dahmer preserved parts of Smith's body.
7. **Curtis Straughter** (April 7, 1990): Straughter, 19, was a young man whom Dahmer lured to his apartment with promises of money. He was killed and dismembered.
8. **Ernest Miller** (September 2, 1990): Miller, 22, was lured to Dahmer's apartment, where he was drugged, killed, and dismembered. Dahmer kept parts of his body.
9. **David Thomas** (June 30, 1990): A 23-year-old male, Thomas was another victim of

Dahmer's killing spree. He was drugged, strangled, and dismembered.

10. **Tony Hughes** (May 31, 1990): Hughes, a 31-year-old aspiring model who was deaf and mute, was lured to Dahmer's apartment. After being drugged and killed, Dahmer preserved parts of his body.
11. **Konerak Sinthasomphone** (May 27, 1990): Sinthasomphone, 14, was drugged, killed, and dismembered. His murder became notorious due to the failure of the police to act on his escape from Dahmer's apartment, which had been reported by neighbors.
12. **Matt Turner** (September 17, 1989): Turner, 21, was another victim of Dahmer. He was lured to Dahmer's apartment, drugged, killed, and dismembered.
13. **Oliver Lacy** (July 15, 1990): Lacy, 23, was an aspiring model. Dahmer lured him to his apartment, where he was drugged, killed, and dismembered. Dahmer kept parts of Lacy's body.
14. **Jeremiah Weinberger** (June 27, 1990): Weinberger, 23, was drugged, killed, and dismembered by Dahmer. His body parts were later discovered in Dahmer's apartment.
15. **Robert Hicks** (October 14, 1991): Hicks, 21, was one of Dahmer's last victims. He was drugged, killed, and dismembered. His body parts were found in Dahmer's apartment when he was arrested.

16. **James Edwards** (July 19, 1991): Edwards, 22, was lured to Dahmer's apartment, where he was drugged, killed, and dismembered.
17. **Rita Isabell** (June 19, 1991): Isabell, a 20-year-old woman, was murdered by Dahmer. Her body was discovered along with other victims in Dahmer's apartment.

Jeffrey Dahmer's victims were chosen based on a mix of factors, including their vulnerability and his own personal preferences. Dahmer's pattern of targeting marginalized individuals, including young men of color and those struggling with addiction, contributed to his ability to evade detection for so long. The horrifying nature of his crimes and the detailed descriptions provided by Dahmer during his confessions have left a lasting impact on the public's understanding of serial killers and the criminal justice system.

Arrest and Investigation

Dahmer's criminal activities went largely undetected for years, despite several warning signs. His arrest came in July 1991, after Tracy Edwards, one of Dahmer's intended victims, managed to escape from his apartment and flagged down two police officers. Edwards led the officers back to Dahmer's apartment, where they discovered photographs of dismembered bodies and human remains.

The discovery of Dahmer's apartment revealed a horrifying array of evidence. Police found severed heads, skulls, and body parts, confirming Edwards' claims and leading to Dahmer's immediate arrest. During his interrogation, Dahmer confessed to the murder of 17 young men and boys, providing detailed accounts of his actions.

The investigation into Dahmer's crimes was extensive, involving the search of his apartment and the examination of evidence. The gruesome nature of the evidence shocked the public and law enforcement officials alike. Dahmer's detailed confessions and the physical evidence presented a clear and horrifying picture of his criminal activities.

Trial and Conviction

Jeffrey Dahmer's trial began in January 1992. The prosecution presented a strong case against him, supported by the overwhelming physical evidence and Dahmer's own confessions. Dahmer's defense team argued that he was suffering from a mental illness, but this strategy was largely unsuccessful.

The trial was a media sensation, drawing widespread attention from reporters, victims' families, and the public. The graphic details of Dahmer's crimes were extensively reported, adding to the shock and horror surrounding the case. Dahmer's demeanor during the trial was calm and detached, which further unsettled the public.

On February 15, 1992, Dahmer was convicted of 15 counts of murder and sentenced to 15 consecutive life terms in prison. He was also sentenced to an additional 70 years for other charges, including sexual assault and necrophilia. The conviction was a significant moment in American legal history, highlighting the severity of Dahmer's crimes and the complexities of criminal psychology.

Imprisonment and Death

Dahmer's imprisonment was marked by significant media attention and public interest. He was housed at the Columbia Correctional Institution in Portage, Wisconsin. Despite his conviction, Dahmer remained a subject of intense fascination and scrutiny.

In November 1994, Dahmer was attacked and killed by a fellow inmate, Christopher Scarver, while performing janitorial work in the prison gymnasium. Scarver, who later claimed that he believed he was carrying out divine justice, fatally bludgeoned Dahmer and another inmate, Jesse Anderson, with a metal bar.

Dahmer's death was a highly publicized event, raising questions about prison safety and the handling of high-profile inmates. The circumstances of his death highlighted the complex dynamics within the prison system and the challenges associated with managing notorious criminals.

Impact and Legacy

The impact of Jeffrey Dahmer's crimes extended far beyond the immediate aftermath of his arrest and trial. The families of his victims experienced immense grief and trauma, and the psychological and emotional scars left by his crimes were deep and lasting. The media coverage of Dahmer's case contributed to a broader societal discussion about violence, mental illness, and the criminal justice system.

Dahmer's case prompted changes in how law enforcement and mental health professionals' approach and investigate serial crimes. The public's reaction to Dahmer's crimes highlighted the need for better mental health support and early intervention to address issues related to criminal behavior.

The Dahmer case also sparked debates about the nature of evil and the limits of human depravity. The shocking details of his crimes challenged conventional understandings of criminality and raised questions about the factors that contribute to such extreme behavior.

Conclusion

Jeffrey Dahmer remains one of the most notorious figures in American criminal history. His heinous crimes, characterized by murder, dismemberment, and cannibalism, continue to shock and horrify. The investigation, trial, and eventual death of Dahmer highlight the complexities of criminal behavior and the challenges faced by law enforcement and the legal system in addressing severe and violent offenses.

Dahmer's life and crimes serve as a grim reminder of the capacity for violence within individuals and the importance of addressing underlying psychological and social issues. The story of Jeffrey Dahmer reflects both the darkness that can exist within individuals and the resilience of those who work to bring justice and healing to affected communities. The legacy of Jeffrey Dahmer's crimes is a sobering reminder of the need for vigilance, empathy, and effective intervention in the face of extreme criminal behavior.

Jeffrey Dahmer

Chapter 5

Walter Ellis

Walter Ellis: The Milwaukee North Side Strangler

Walter Ellis, infamously known as the Milwaukee North Side Strangler, is a notorious figure in the annals of American crime. His reign of terror, spanning from the late 1980s to the early 2000s, resulted in the brutal murders of at least seven women. Ellis's gruesome crimes left a lasting mark on the Milwaukee community and have been the subject of intense investigation and media coverage. This account delves into his life, his crimes, and the impact he left on the city of Milwaukee.

Early Life and Background

Walter Ellis was born on May 20, 1963, in Milwaukee, Wisconsin. Growing up in a troubled household, Ellis's early years were marked by instability and hardship. Raised by his mother, he experienced a turbulent childhood with frequent moves and economic struggles. The lack of a stable home environment, combined with other underlying factors, contributed to the development of his later criminal behavior.

As a young adult, Ellis faced numerous legal issues, including petty crimes and misdemeanors. He was often in and out of jail, but these infractions were relatively minor compared to the horrific crimes he would later commit. Despite these early brushes with the law, Ellis managed to maintain a semblance of normalcy in his life. He worked various low-paying jobs and lived in different neighborhoods around Milwaukee, including the North Side, where his reign of terror would unfold.

The Emergence of a Serial Killer

Ellis's transition from petty criminal to serial killer was gradual and disturbing. His first known victim was identified in 1986, and over the next decade, he would go on to commit a series of brutal murders. The victims, all women, were found strangled, often with their own clothing or other items. The consistent pattern of his killings led to his moniker, the Milwaukee North Side Strangler.

Ellis's modus operandi involved luring his victims, often under the guise of offering them assistance or companionship. Once in his control, he would strangle them and leave their bodies in secluded areas. His ability to evade capture for so long was partly due to the lack of a clear motive or pattern that would immediately connect the murders. The killings were initially seen as isolated incidents, and it took years for law enforcement to link them together.

Victims:

Walter Ellis, the Milwaukee North Side Strangler, was responsible for the murders of at least seven women in Milwaukee, Wisconsin, between 1986 and 2007. His victims were targeted in a series of brutal attacks that shocked the community and led to a prolonged investigation. Here is a detailed list of his known victims:

1. **Gloria Bobo** (1986): Gloria Bobo, 26 years old, was one of Ellis's earliest victims. She was found strangled in her apartment. Her death was initially classified as a natural occurrence due to the lack of immediate forensic evidence linking it to a serial killer.
2. **Yvonne Cottom** (1994): Yvonne Cottom, 44 years old, was found dead in her home. She had been strangled, and the case went unsolved for years until Ellis was eventually linked to her murder through DNA evidence.
3. **Dawn H.** (1994): The name of the victim is often reported as "Dawn H." due to privacy concerns. She was 32 years old when she was killed. Her body was discovered in a secluded area, and she had been strangled.
4. **Patricia Smith** (2000): Patricia Smith, 36 years old, was found strangled in her apartment. Her death was one of the later murders attributed to Ellis, and it helped to

link his crimes together through forensic evidence.
5. **Lynette "Lynn" M.** (2002): Lynette M., 39 years old, was found strangled in her home. Her murder was part of the series that eventually led to Ellis's capture.
6. **Janelle Smith** (2004): Janelle Smith, 27 years old, was found dead under similar circumstances as the other victims. Her murder further cemented Ellis's pattern of targeting women and strangling them.
7. **Cynthia "Cindy" Williams** (2007): Cynthia Williams, 35 years old, was Ellis's last known victim before his arrest. Her murder was linked to Ellis through DNA evidence, leading to his capture and conviction.

These victims were all women living in Milwaukee's North Side, and their murders were characterized by a similar modus operandi: strangulation with items such as clothing or cords. Ellis's crimes were marked by their brutality and the fear they instilled in the community. The investigation into his crimes was prolonged, but the eventual capture of Ellis and his conviction provided a measure of closure for the victims' families and the community at large.

The Investigation and Capture

The investigation into the Milwaukee North Side Strangler began in earnest in the early 1990s. The Milwaukee Police Department, working with the FBI, conducted an extensive and exhaustive search for the perpetrator. They scrutinized numerous suspects and conducted numerous interviews, but for years, Ellis remained a shadowy figure in the background of the investigation.

Ellis's eventual capture was the result of a combination of forensic advancements and diligent police work. In 2009, the case took a significant turn when DNA evidence linked Ellis to several of the murders. The breakthrough came after years of painstaking work by investigators who had kept the case files active despite numerous dead ends.

Ellis was arrested in September 2009 at his home. The arrest followed a painstaking investigation that involved re-examining evidence, re-interviewing witnesses, and using modern forensic techniques to link Ellis to the crimes. The DNA evidence was crucial in securing his arrest and subsequent conviction. It was a significant moment for the victims' families and the community, providing a sense of closure after years of uncertainty.

The Trial and Conviction

Walter Ellis's trial was a highly anticipated event, attracting significant media attention. The trial, which began in 2010, was marked by intense courtroom drama. Ellis faced multiple charges, including first-degree murder, and the prosecution presented a compelling case against him.

During the trial, the prosecution highlighted the forensic evidence linking Ellis to the murders, including DNA found on the victims. They also presented testimony from witnesses who had seen Ellis in the vicinity of the crime scenes. The defense attempted to challenge the evidence and argue for Ellis's innocence, but the overwhelming weight of the prosecution's case proved insurmountable.

In 2010, Ellis was convicted of multiple counts of first-degree murder. The jury's verdict was met with relief by the victims' families and the Milwaukee community. The sentencing phase of the trial saw Ellis receive multiple life sentences without the possibility of parole. The sentences were a testament to the severity of his crimes and a measure of justice for the victims.

The Impact on the Community

The impact of Ellis's crimes on the Milwaukee community was profound. The North Side, where many of the murders took place, was left reeling from the shock and fear caused by the killings. The sense of safety and security that residents had taken for granted was shattered, and the community faced the challenges of coping with the trauma and loss caused by Ellis's actions.

The murders also highlighted issues related to violence against women, and Ellis's case became a focal point for discussions about improving the response to such crimes. The extensive media coverage of the case brought national attention to the issue, prompting calls for increased resources and support for victims of violence.

In the aftermath of Ellis's capture and conviction, efforts were made to support the victims' families and provide resources for those affected by the crimes. Community organizations and advocacy groups worked to address the issues highlighted by the case and to support survivors and families impacted by violence.

Reflections and Legacy

Walter Ellis's story is a stark reminder of the devastating impact of serial violence. His crimes left a lasting scar on the Milwaukee community, and his case remains a subject of interest for those studying criminal psychology and forensic science. The investigation and capture of Ellis were significant achievements for law enforcement, showcasing the advancements in forensic techniques and the persistence of investigators.

Ellis's legacy is one of horror and tragedy, but it also serves as a reminder of the resilience of communities in the face of adversity. The response to his crimes, both in terms of the investigation and the support for the victims' families, highlights the importance of justice and the ongoing efforts to address violence in society.

In summary, Walter Ellis, the Milwaukee North Side Strangler, is a figure whose crimes have left a profound impact on the community and on the field of criminal justice. His story, marked by brutality and the eventual triumph of justice, serves as a chilling reminder of the darker aspects of human nature and the ongoing need for vigilance and support in addressing violent crime.

Walter Ellis

Chapter 6

Steven Zelich

In June 2014, the community of Walworth County, Wisconsin, was stunned when the bodies of two women were found stuffed inside suitcases by a highway. The unfortunate discovery led the police to investigate missing person reports, eventually identifying the victims as Laura Simonson and Jenny Gamez. Investigation Discovery's 'Web of Lies: In Dark Corners' chronicles how, the killer met the women online through bondage websites and then murdered them. So, let's find out more about this case then, shall we?

How Did Laura Simonson and Jenny Gamez Die?

Laura Simonson was born in March 1976 and lived in Farmington, Minnesota. The loving mother of seven was reported missing by her mother on November 22, 2013, and the 37-year-old was last seen about twenty days prior. Jenny, on the other hand, was from Cottage Grove, Oregon. After finishing high school, the 19-year-old attended community college before moving to California with friends.

Laura Simonson   Jenny Gamez

At the time of Jenny's disappearance in 2012, she told people she was moving to Milwaukee to study welding. In a sad turn of events, Laura and Jenny would be found together, dead. On June 5, 2014, workers on a highway in Walworth County discovered suitcases by the side of the road while cutting grass. The authorities later confirmed the decomposing remains to be Laura and Jenny's. One of the bodies was found naked, with a gag ball in her mouth.

Who Killed Laura Simonson and Jenny Gamez?

The authorities learned that Laura had been missing for about seven months. She was last seen at a motel in Rochester, Minnesota, on November 2, 2013. The employees recognized her from the missing person reports and told the police that she had been there with another man. While the two checked in together on November 2, the man left alone the next day. This person was identified as Steven Zelich, a former police officer working in the security industry at the time.

Steven quit the force months after a sex worker claimed that a struggle ensued while she was leaving Steven's home. The ex-officer stated that the woman tried to steal from him. Furthermore, it was reported that Steven went to strip clubs while on duty and had apparently asked a dancer out about 1000 times over eight years. Just weeks after the bodies were discovered, physical evidence connected Steven to the dead bodies.

After being arrested, Steven admitted that he met the women online through websites catered to bondage fetish. Steven claimed that after meeting Jenny, he invited her to visit Wisconsin and picked her up from the airport. Then, they checked into a motel in Kenosha, Wisconsin, where they stayed for several days. Over there, the two indulged in erotic asphyxiation. While playing a sexual game called "breath play," Steven claimed to have lost control and choked her to death in August 2012. More than a year later, Laura was killed under similar circumstances in Rochester.

Steven then confessed to bringing the bodies back to his apartment and keeping them in the refrigerator. In Jenny's case, he had her for over a year. Steven then put the remains in his car before dumping them off by the highway in June 2014. An ex-roommate of his stated that he once told her a disturbing secret, adding, "He said that he kept a girl for seven years in his apartment, in this crate, this cage, and he would leave there during the day when he went to work as a police officer, and he would come home on lunch and check in on her."

The authorities had further evidence that he was in conversation with another woman online and planned to recruit her as a "permanent slave to live with him" around the same time he disposed of Jenny and Laura's remains. The prosecution claimed that Steven preyed on vulnerable women and used his experience as a police officer to his advantage while committing the murders. However, the defense argued that the deaths were accidental and occurred during consensual sexual activity.

Where is Steven Zelich Now?

Steven first pleaded guilty to first-degree reckless homicide and hiding a corpse in Jenny's death in Wisconsin. In March 2016, he received 35 years for reckless homicide and a concurrent-three-year term for hiding a corpse. Then, in February 2017, Steven, then 55 years old, pleaded guilty to second-degree murder with intent for killing Laura in Minnesota. For that, he received a 25-year sentence that would be served after finishing his term in Wisconsin. Finally, in late 2017, Steven was convicted on two counts of hiding a corpse in Walworth County and was handed down two consecutive five-year terms. Prison records indicate that he remains incarcerated at Dodge Correctional Institution in Waupun, Wisconsin.

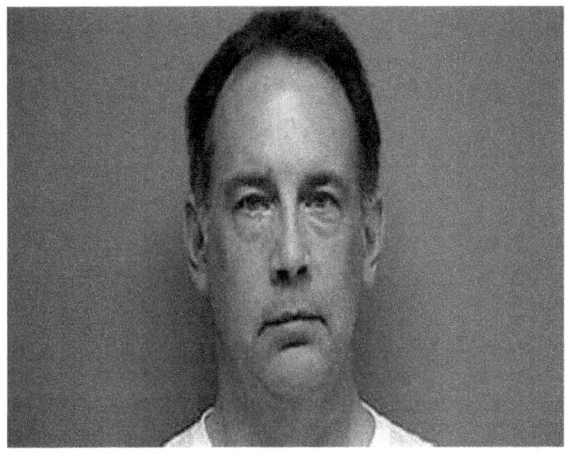

Steven Zelich

Chapter 7

Ashlee Martinson

Ashlee Martinson, often referred to as the "Horrorcore Killer," is a young woman whose case garnered significant media attention due to the brutal nature of her crimes and the disturbing circumstances surrounding her life. Born on March 6, 1998, in Rhinelander, Wisconsin, Ashlee's early life was marked by turmoil and abuse, factors that played a crucial role in the tragic events that unfolded in 2015.

Early Life and Background

Ashlee Martinson's childhood was far from idyllic. She grew up in a troubled household where abuse was a constant presence. Her biological father was abusive, and her mother, Jennifer Ayers, struggled with her own issues, leading to a volatile family environment. Jennifer later remarried Thomas Ayers, who, according to Ashlee, was also abusive and controlling. This environment of fear and oppression had a profound impact on Ashlee's psychological well-being.

From a young age, Ashlee found solace in writing and dark poetry, often expressing her feelings of anger, pain, and isolation through her creative works. She was an avid reader of horror literature and became fascinated with the macabre, earning her the nickname "Vampchick" online. Her writings and online presence, however, would later be scrutinized and used against her in court.

The Murders

On March 7, 2015, a day after her 17th birthday, Ashlee Martinson committed a double homicide that shocked the small community of Piehl, Wisconsin. In a gruesome attack, she murdered her mother, Jennifer Ayers, and stepfather, Thomas Ayers, in their home. The details of the crime were horrifying:

- **Jennifer Ayers**: Ashlee shot her mother in the head at close range. Jennifer's body was found in the living room, indicating a sudden and brutal end.
- **Thomas Ayers**: After killing her mother, Ashlee turned her attention to her stepfather. She stabbed Thomas more than 30 times with a hunting knife. His body was found in a bedroom, suggesting a frenzied and rage-fueled attack.

After committing the murders, Ashlee locked her three younger siblings, aged 2, 8, and 9, in a bedroom to protect them from the carnage. She then fled the scene, initiating a manhunt that would end with her capture in Indiana, nearly 700 miles away.

The Investigation and Trial

The investigation into the murders revealed a troubled teenager who had endured years of abuse and had become increasingly detached from reality. Ashlee's online writings and social media posts were examined, painting a picture of a girl who felt trapped and desperate.

During her trial, Ashlee pleaded guilty to second-degree intentional homicide as part of a plea deal. This agreement spared her the possibility of a life sentence without parole, which would have been likely if she had been convicted of first-degree intentional homicide. Instead, she received a sentence of 23 years in prison followed by 17 years of extended supervision.

Motive and Psychological Evaluation

The case raised numerous questions about Ashlee's mental state and the extent to which her abusive upbringing contributed to her actions. Psychological evaluations conducted during the trial suggested that Ashlee suffered from post-traumatic stress disorder (PTSD) and depression, conditions that were exacerbated by the abuse she experienced at the hands of her stepfather.

Her defense team argued that years of abuse had left Ashlee feeling hopeless and pushed her to the breaking point. They contended that the murders were a desperate attempt to escape a life of pain and fear. The prosecution, however, highlighted the premeditated nature of the killings, pointing to the fact that Ashlee had written about wanting to kill her parents before the incident occurred.

Aftermath and Public Perception

The Ashlee Martinson case sparked a debate about the intersection of abuse, mental health, and criminal responsibility. Many people saw Ashlee as a victim who was driven to commit an unthinkable act because of her traumatic upbringing. Others viewed her as a cold-blooded killer who could have sought help instead of resorting to violence.

Her case also brought attention to the phenomenon of "horrorcore" and its potential influence on vulnerable individuals. Horrorcore is a subgenre of hip-hop music characterized by its explicit and often violent lyrics. While there is no direct evidence that horrorcore music played a role in Ashlee's actions, her fascination with dark themes and horror imagery became a focal point in discussions about her state of mind.

Conclusion

The story of Ashlee Martinson is a tragic example of how a combination of abuse, mental illness, and isolation can lead to devastating consequences. Her case underscores the importance of addressing the root causes of violence and providing support to individuals who are suffering from trauma and abuse.

Ashlee Martinson's life took a dark turn that resulted in the loss of two lives and left a community in shock. While she will spend a significant portion of her life in prison, her story serves as a reminder of the complex interplay between personal trauma and criminal behavior, and the need for a compassionate and nuanced approach to justice and rehabilitation.

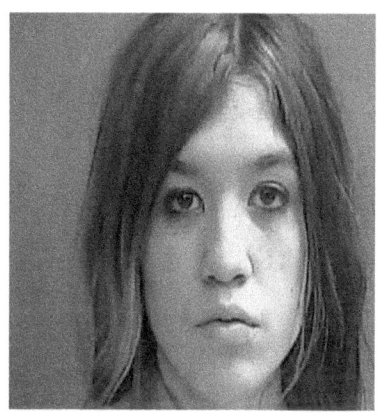

Ashlee Martinson

Chapter 8

Steven Avery

Steven Avery's story is a complex and controversial one, spanning decades and involving multiple convictions, exonerations, and a high-profile documentary series. Here is an in-depth exploration of his life and legal battles.

Early Life

Steven Allan Avery was born on July 9, 1962, in Manitowoc County, Wisconsin. He grew up in a rural area on his family's 40-acre salvage yard. Avery's family was not wealthy, and he had a troubled childhood, marked by struggles in school and with the law. He was known to have a low IQ and learning disabilities, which contributed to his difficulties in life.

The 1985 Conviction

In 1985, Avery was convicted of sexual assault and attempted murder. The victim, Penny Beerntsen, a local woman, was jogging on a beach near Two Rivers, Wisconsin, when she was brutally attacked. Based on her identification and other circumstantial evidence, Avery was arrested and charged with the crime. Despite having an alibi supported by numerous witnesses, Avery was convicted and sentenced to 32 years in prison.

Penny Beernsten

Exoneration and Release

Avery maintained his innocence throughout his incarceration. In the early 2000s, with the advent of DNA testing, the Wisconsin Innocence Project took up his case. In 2003, DNA evidence proved that Avery was not the perpetrator. Instead, it pointed to Gregory Allen, a known sex offender who had committed similar crimes in the area. After serving 18 years in prison, Avery was exonerated and released.

The Civil Suit

Following his exoneration, Avery filed a $36 million lawsuit against Manitowoc County, the former sheriff, and the district attorney, alleging wrongful conviction and imprisonment. The suit was poised to bring significant scrutiny to the county and law enforcement practices, and it seemed that Avery's life was finally taking a turn for the better. However, this period of hope was short-lived.

The Teresa Halbach Case

In October 2005, Teresa Halbach, a 25-year-old photographer, went missing. She had been last seen at the Avery Salvage Yard, where she was photographing a vehicle for Auto Trader magazine. Her charred remains were later found on the property. Avery was quickly arrested and charged with her murder.

Teresa Halbach

The Trial and Conviction

The trial, which began in early 2007, was a media sensation. Avery's defense team argued that he had been framed by law enforcement officials seeking to discredit his wrongful conviction lawsuit. They pointed to numerous inconsistencies and procedural errors in the investigation, including the handling of evidence.

Despite these arguments, Avery was found guilty of first-degree murder and illegal possession of a firearm by a felon. He was sentenced to life in prison without the possibility of parole. His nephew, Brendan Dassey, who was also implicated in the crime, was convicted of being a party to first-degree murder, mutilation of a corpse, and second-degree sexual assault.

Brendan Dassey

"Making a Murderer"

In 2015, Netflix released the documentary series "Making a Murderer," which chronicled Avery's story and raised questions about the fairness of his trial. The series suggested that Avery was the victim of a corrupt justice system and sparked a public outcry, leading to widespread calls for a re-examination of the case.

The series highlighted several key issues:

1. **Conflict of Interest**: Manitowoc County officials were involved in the investigation despite the ongoing lawsuit, raising questions about bias and conflict of interest.
2. **Evidence Handling**: The discovery of key pieces of evidence, such as Halbach's car key and Avery's blood in her vehicle, was highly suspicious. The defense argued that these items had been planted to frame Avery.
3. **Brendan Dassey's Confession**: Dassey's confession, obtained through questionable interrogation techniques, was a major point of contention. Critics argued that his rights had been violated and that his confession was coerced.
4.

Legal Battles Post-Conviction

Following the release of "Making a Murderer," Avery and Dassey's legal teams continued to fight for their release. Dassey's case received particular attention, with his legal team arguing that his confession was involuntary and should be thrown out.

In 2016, a federal judge ruled that Dassey's confession had been coerced and ordered his release. However, this decision was later overturned by an appellate court, and the U.S. Supreme Court declined to hear his case. Dassey remains in prison, serving his life sentence.

Avery's legal team, led by high-profile attorney Kathleen Zellner, has filed multiple appeals and motions for a new trial. Zellner has presented new evidence and expert testimony that she claims exonerates Avery and points to other potential suspects. Despite these efforts, Avery remains in prison, with his appeals being repeatedly denied.

Public Reaction and Impact

The "Making a Murderer" series brought Avery's case to the forefront of public consciousness, sparking debates about the criminal justice system, police corruption, and wrongful convictions. The series drew a global audience and led to numerous petitions and campaigns advocating for Avery and Dassey's release.

Critics of the series argue that it was biased and omitted key evidence that pointed to Avery's guilt. They contend that the documentary misled viewers and painted an incomplete picture of the case. Supporters, on the other hand, believe that Avery and Dassey are innocent and that they were railroaded by a corrupt system.

Continuing Developments

The fight for justice in Avery's case continues, with new developments and legal maneuvers emerging regularly. Kathleen Zellner remains committed to proving Avery's innocence and has filed multiple motions presenting new evidence and witnesses.

In 2019, Zellner filed a motion for a new trial, citing new evidence that she claimed undermined the prosecution's case. This included advanced DNA testing methods that she argued could prove Avery's innocence. The motion was denied, but Zellner has continued to pursue other legal avenues.

Broader Implications

Avery's case has had a significant impact on public awareness of wrongful convictions and the criminal justice system. It has highlighted the potential for bias, misconduct, and errors in the legal process, and has underscored the importance of ongoing scrutiny and reform.

The case has also prompted discussions about the role of media in shaping public perception of criminal cases. "Making a Murderer" demonstrated the power of documentary filmmaking in bringing attention to legal injustices, but it also raised questions about the responsibilities of filmmakers in presenting balanced and accurate accounts.

Conclusion

The story of Steven Avery is a complex and ongoing saga that raises important questions about justice, truth, and the American legal system. It is a story of a man who has spent most of his life behind bars, maintaining his innocence in the face of overwhelming legal battles and public scrutiny.

Whether Avery is truly guilty or the victim of a grave miscarriage of justice remains a topic of heated debate. What is clear, however, is that his case has had a profound impact on the way we view the criminal justice system and the potential for error and corruption within it.

As the legal battles continue and new evidence emerges, the story of Steven Avery remains a powerful reminder of the importance of vigilance, fairness, and the relentless pursuit of truth in the quest for justice.

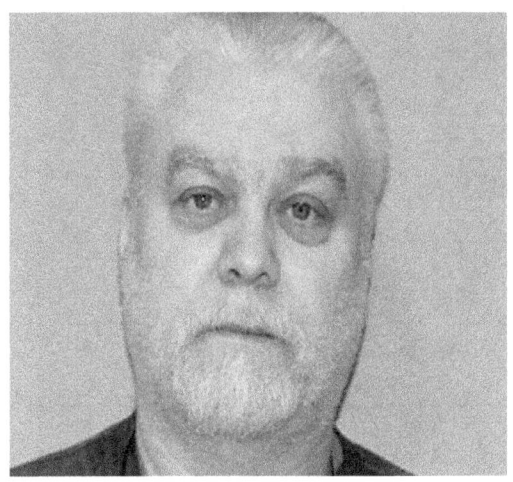

Steven Avery

Chapter 9

Joseph Paul Franklin

Joseph Paul Franklin, born James Clayton Vaughn Jr. on April 13, 1950, in Mobile, Alabama, was a notorious American serial killer, neo-Nazi, and white supremacist. He is best known for his racially motivated killing spree that took place across the United States between 1977 and 1980. Franklin's violent rampage, driven by a virulent hatred of African Americans, Jews, and interracial couples, left at least 22 people dead, although he later claimed responsibility for many more attacks. His story is one of deep-seated racism, a turbulent early life, and a chilling series of murders that spanned several states.

Early Life and Ideological Radicalization

Joseph Paul Franklin's early life was marred by instability, violence, and a dysfunctional family environment. His father abandoned the family when he was eight years old, leaving his mother to raise him and his siblings in poverty. Franklin dropped out of school in the ninth grade, and by his late teens, he had become deeply involved in white supremacist and neo-Nazi ideologies.

Franklin's radicalization began with his exposure to the writings of figures like George Lincoln Rockwell, the founder of the American Nazi Party, and other white supremacist literature. He legally changed his name to Joseph Paul Franklin, inspired by Paul Joseph Goebbels, the Nazi propaganda minister, and Benjamin Franklin, one of America's Founding Fathers. This name change symbolized his commitment to his extremist beliefs.

The Killing Spree Begins

Franklin's killing spree began in 1977 and was marked by a series of calculated and racially motivated attacks. His primary targets were African Americans, Jews, and interracial couples. He believed that by killing people who represented these groups, he could incite a race war and purify the United States.

One of Franklin's first known attacks occurred on July 29, 1977, when he fired five shots at a group of black men from his car in Liberty City, a predominantly African American neighborhood in Miami, Florida. No one was killed in this attack, but it set the stage for the violence that would follow.

In August 1977, Franklin committed his first known murder. He traveled to a synagogue in Richmond Heights, Missouri, where he shot and killed a prominent Jewish businessman, Alphonse Manning, and his teenage daughter, Toni. This double murder demonstrated Franklin's willingness to target innocent individuals simply because of their race and religion.

The Wisconsin Murders

Wisconsin was one of the states where Franklin left a bloody mark. His killing spree in the state is particularly notable for its brutality and the racially charged motivations behind the attacks.

The Milwaukee Murders

In August 1977, Franklin traveled to Milwaukee, Wisconsin, where he shot and killed a young interracial couple, Alfred and Bernice Reitler, as they exited a fast-food restaurant. This murder was part of Franklin's broader campaign against interracial relationships, which he viewed as an abomination. The Reitler murder shocked the Milwaukee community and underscored the deadly consequences of Franklin's racist ideology.

The Rampage Intensifies

Franklin's killing spree continued throughout 1978, with several high-profile and brutal attacks. On October 8, 1978, he gunned down a young interracial couple, Jesse Taylor and Marian Bresette, in Oklahoma City. Franklin had a particular hatred for interracial relationships, viewing them as a threat to white purity.

In July 1979, Franklin escalated his campaign of terror by bombing a synagogue in Chattanooga, Tennessee. Although no one was killed in the explosion, it caused significant damage and heightened fears within the Jewish community. Franklin later claimed responsibility for the bombing, expressing satisfaction at the destruction he had caused.

On July 29, 1979, Franklin shot and killed a black man, Harold McIver, in Doraville, Georgia. McIver was walking home from a convenience store when Franklin approached him and opened fire. This murder was part of Franklin's broader strategy to instill fear in African American communities.

The Murders of 1980

The year 1980 marked the peak of Franklin's killing spree, with several high-profile attacks and murders. On May 29, 1980, he shot and killed two young black boys, cousins Darrell Lane and Dante Evans Brown, in Cincinnati, Ohio. The boys were walking home from a convenience store when Franklin ambushed them. This senseless act of violence shocked the local community and underscored Franklin's utter lack of remorse.

On June 8, 1980, Franklin targeted an interracial couple, Arthur Smothers and Kathleen Mikula, in Johnstown, Pennsylvania. He shot and killed Smothers, a black man, and seriously wounded Mikula, a white woman. Franklin's obsession with interracial relationships continued to drive his violent actions.

The Assassination of Vernon Jordan

One of Franklin's most notorious attacks occurred on May 29, 1980, when he attempted to assassinate civil rights leader Vernon Jordan in Fort Wayne, Indiana. Jordan, the president of the National Urban League, was shot in the back with a high-powered rifle but miraculously survived. This attack brought Franklin to the attention of the FBI, who launched a nationwide manhunt for the elusive killer.

Franklin's ability to evade capture was partly due to his transient lifestyle. He traveled extensively, living out of motels, using fake identities, and frequently changing his appearance. His meticulous planning and ability to blend into different communities made him a difficult target for law enforcement.

Capture and Conviction

Franklin's luck ran out on October 28, 1980, when he was arrested in a blood bank in Lakeland, Florida. A sharp-eyed employee recognized him from a wanted poster and alerted the authorities. Franklin was apprehended without incident, bringing an end to his three-year killing spree.

Once in custody, Franklin confessed to a litany of crimes, proudly detailing his racially motivated attacks and murders. His confessions led to a series of trials across multiple states, resulting in numerous convictions and life sentences. Despite the overwhelming evidence against him, Franklin remained unrepentant, viewing his actions as part of a larger mission to purify America.

Execution and Legacy

Joseph Paul Franklin was sentenced to death for the murder of Gerald Gordon, a Jewish man whom he had killed in 1977 outside a synagogue in St. Louis, Missouri. After years of legal appeals and delays, Franklin was executed by lethal injection on November 20, 2013, at the age of 63.

Franklin's legacy is one of hatred, violence, and the devastating impact of extremist ideologies. His killing spree highlighted the dangers posed by individuals driven by racist and anti-Semitic beliefs, and it underscored the need for vigilance and proactive measures to counteract such threats.

Psychological Profile

Understanding Franklin's psychological profile offers insights into the mind of a serial killer fueled by ideological extremism. Franklin exhibited traits consistent with psychopathy, including a lack of empathy, a penchant for violence, and a grandiose sense of purpose. His actions were driven by a deeply ingrained belief in white supremacy and a desire to incite a race war.

Franklin's background, marked by childhood abuse, poverty, and educational struggles, likely contributed to his radicalization. His early exposure to extremist literature and white supremacist groups provided a framework for his violent actions. Unlike many serial killers driven by personal compulsion, Franklin's murders were ideologically motivated, making him a unique and particularly dangerous figure in the annals of American criminal history.

Societal Impact

Franklin's killing spree had a profound impact on the communities he terrorized and on the broader American society. His racially motivated violence highlighted the persistent threat of domestic terrorism driven by white supremacist ideologies. The fear and trauma experienced by the victims' families and the targeted communities underscored the human cost of such extremist beliefs.

Law enforcement agencies across the United States were forced to confront the reality of ideologically driven serial killers. Franklin's case prompted a reevaluation of investigative techniques and the importance of inter-agency cooperation in tracking and apprehending mobile and transient criminals.

Media and Public Perception

The media coverage of Franklin's crimes and subsequent trials played a significant role in shaping public perception of his actions. His story was covered extensively in newspapers, television news programs, and true crime documentaries, bringing attention to the issue of racially motivated violence in America.

Franklin's case also sparked debates about the death penalty, mental health, and the role of extremist ideologies in fueling violence. His execution, after years of legal battles, reignited discussions about the ethics and effectiveness of capital punishment in deterring heinous crimes.

Conclusion

Joseph Paul Franklin's story is a chilling reminder of the destructive power of hatred and the impact of extremist ideologies. His racially motivated killing spree, spanning several states and claiming numerous lives, left a lasting scar on the American psyche. Franklin's actions were driven by a warped sense of purpose, rooted in a deeply ingrained belief in white supremacy.

The legacy of Franklin's crimes continues to resonate, highlighting the importance of combating racism, anti-Semitism, and all forms of extremist ideologies. His story serves as a cautionary tale, reminding us of the need for vigilance, empathy, and a commitment to justice in the face of hatred and violence. The communities and families affected by Franklin's actions continue to grapple with the trauma and loss he inflicted, underscoring the enduring human cost of his violent rampage.

Joseph Paul Franklin

Chapter 10

Gerald Turner

Gerald Turner, infamously known as the "Halloween Killer," committed one of the most notorious crimes in Wisconsin's history, shocking the community and leaving an enduring scar on the collective memory of the state. His brutal crime on Halloween night in 1973 has haunted Wisconsin for decades, serving as a grim reminder of the potential for darkness even in the most seemingly innocent of settings.

Early Life and Background

Gerald Turner was born in 1949 and raised in the state of Wisconsin. While much of his early life remains obscured by his later infamy, it is known that Turner had a relatively unremarkable childhood and adolescence. He managed to stay out of significant trouble and eventually found employment at a local paper mill in Fond du Lac, Wisconsin. His neighbors and acquaintances described him as quiet and somewhat withdrawn, but not particularly alarming or suspicious.

By 1973, Turner was living with his girlfriend, Arlene Penn, and her children. Despite his unassuming exterior, there were undercurrents of disturbing behavior that hinted at the dark potential within him.

The Crime

On Halloween night in 1973, nine-year-old Lisa Ann French set out to go trick-or-treating in her neighborhood of Fond du Lac. She was dressed in a hobo costume, excited to collect candy with her friends. Little did anyone know; this innocent activity would lead to a night of horror.

Lisa visited several houses before she arrived at Gerald Turner's home. Turner, who had earlier expressed disdain for Halloween, claiming it to be an annoyance, would later reveal a much darker intention. Luring Lisa inside, Turner committed unspeakable acts of violence. He sexually assaulted and subsequently murdered the young girl in a crime so heinous it defies comprehension.

After the attack, Turner placed Lisa's lifeless body into a garbage bag and disposed of it in a rural area outside of town. Her body was discovered the next day, leading to an outpouring of grief and horror from the community. The brutal nature of the crime sent shockwaves through Fond du Lac and beyond, marking the end of an era of perceived safety and innocence in the small town.

The Investigation

The investigation into Lisa Ann French's murder was intense and exhaustive. Fond du Lac police worked tirelessly to track down the killer, piecing together clues and interviewing numerous potential suspects. Despite their efforts, it was a tip from an anonymous source that eventually led them to Gerald Turner.

Turner initially denied any involvement in the crime. However, after a lengthy interrogation and mounting evidence, including forensic analysis linking him to the crime scene, he confessed to the horrific acts he had committed. His detailed confession described the brutal and calculated nature of the crime, leaving no doubt as to his culpability.

Trial and Conviction

Turner's trial was a highly publicized event, drawing significant media attention due to the brutal nature of the crime and the age of the victim. The prosecution presented a strong case, highlighting the overwhelming evidence against Turner, including his own confession. The defense attempted to argue mitigating circumstances, but their efforts were largely overshadowed by the gravity of the crime.

In 1975, Gerald Turner was convicted of first-degree murder, sexual assault, and indecent liberties with a child. He was sentenced to 38 years and six months in prison. The relatively lenient sentence, given the nature of the crime, caused considerable outrage among the public, who felt that justice had not been fully served.

Parole and Public Outcry

Turner's case continued to haunt the public conscience long after his conviction. In 1992, after serving 17 years of his sentence, Turner became eligible for parole under Wisconsin law. The possibility of his release sparked widespread outrage and fear within the community, especially among those who remembered the brutal details of his crime.

In a controversial decision, Turner was granted parole in 1998, prompting a public outcry and a legal battle. The state of Wisconsin passed "Turner's Law," aimed at keeping violent sexual offenders incarcerated beyond their initial sentences if they were deemed a continuing threat to society. This law highlighted the evolving understanding of the need to protect communities from individuals with a high risk of reoffending.

Turner's time as a free man was short-lived. He was returned to prison for violating the terms of his parole and for possessing pornography. He was later re-sentenced to additional time in prison under the newly enacted civil commitment law, which allowed the state to keep him incarcerated due to the continued danger he posed.

Legacy and Impact

The case of Gerald Turner had a profound impact on the state of Wisconsin and the United States as a whole. It led to significant changes in the laws regarding sexual offenders and parole eligibility, highlighting the need for a more robust system to deal with individuals convicted of violent crimes. Turner's crime also brought attention to the importance of community safety and the need for vigilance, especially during events like Halloween, which were previously seen as entirely safe for children.

The murder of Lisa Ann French remains a poignant and painful memory for those who lived through it. Each Halloween, her story is often recounted, serving as both a tribute to her short life and a stark reminder of the potential dangers that lurk in the shadows. Community efforts to honor Lisa's memory include vigils and the establishment of safety programs aimed at protecting children from similar fates.

Psychological Profile

Gerald Turner's crime has also been the subject of numerous psychological analyses. Experts have attempted to understand what could drive an individual to commit such a horrific act. Turner's background did not suggest a history of severe mental illness or significant behavioral problems, making his crime even more perplexing.

Some psychologists have suggested that Turner may have harbored deep-seated anger and resentment, possibly stemming from personal failures or frustrations. His decision to target an innocent child on Halloween night indicates a level of premeditation and a desire to exert power and control in a situation where he felt dominant. This psychological profile underscores the unpredictable nature of violent offenders and the challenges in predicting and preventing such crimes.

Turner's Current Status

As of now, Gerald Turner remains incarcerated. His repeated attempts for release have been met with strong resistance from both the legal system and the public. Turner's case continues to be cited in discussions about the handling of sexual offenders and the balance between rehabilitation and public safety.

His continued incarceration is seen by many as a necessary measure to protect the community, given the brutal nature of his crime and the enduring trauma it inflicted on Lisa Ann French's family and the community of Fond du Lac. The legacy of his crime has ensured that his name remains synonymous with one of the darkest chapters in Wisconsin's history.

Conclusion

The story of Gerald Turner, the Halloween Killer, is a grim chapter in Wisconsin's history. His brutal murder of Lisa Ann French on Halloween night in 1973 shattered the sense of safety and innocence in the small town of Fond du Lac and left an indelible mark on the community. Turner's crime and the subsequent legal battles over his parole eligibility highlighted significant gaps in the justice system's ability to protect the public from dangerous offenders.

Turner's case led to important legislative changes aimed at keeping violent sexual offenders incarcerated and protecting communities from their potential recidivism. His repeated attempts for parole and the public outcry that followed underscored the ongoing struggle between rehabilitation and public safety in the criminal justice system.

Despite the passage of time, the memory of Lisa Ann French and the horror of her murder remain vivid. Turner's crime continues to serve as a cautionary tale and a reminder of the importance of vigilance, community safety, and the need for a justice system that can effectively balance the rights of offenders with the safety of the public. The legacy of Gerald Turner's crime is a somber reminder of the darkness that can exist within individuals and the enduring impact of their actions on the lives of others.

Gerald Turner

Chapter 11

Chai Vang

The story of Chai Vang and the tragic events that unfolded in the Wisconsin woods in November 2004 is a chilling narrative that underscores the volatility that can arise from a combination of cultural misunderstandings, intense emotions, and the presence of firearms. This incident, often referred to as the Chai Vang murders, resulted in the deaths of six individuals and left two others seriously injured. It is a tale of hunting gone horribly wrong, leading to one of the most notorious mass murders in Wisconsin's history.

Background

Chai Vang was a Hmong immigrant who had come to the United States from Laos in the 1980s. The Hmong people, originally from Southeast Asia, were recruited by the CIA during the Vietnam War to fight against communist forces. After the war, many Hmong families, including Vang's, resettled in the United States to escape persecution.

By 2004, Vang, a naturalized U.S. citizen, was living in St. Paul, Minnesota. He was an experienced hunter, familiar with the woods and accustomed to the practices and traditions of hunting, which held cultural significance for him and many other Hmong immigrants. However, hunting in the United States also involved navigating property rights and regulations, which sometimes created tension between Hmong hunters and local landowners.

The Incident

On November 21, 2004, during the deer hunting season, Chai Vang was hunting alone in the woods of northern Wisconsin, near the town of Meteor in Sawyer County. During his hunt, he unknowingly trespassed onto private property owned by Terry Willers and occupied by a group of hunting companions. When Willers and another member of the group, Lauren Hesebeck, noticed Vang in a deer stand on their property, they approached him and asked him to leave.

A confrontation ensued, which quickly escalated into a violent and deadly encounter. According to court testimonies and later reports, there was a heated exchange of words, and Vang claimed that racial slurs were directed at him. As Vang began to leave, one of the hunters, Terry Willers, allegedly fired a shot at him. This initial shot missed, but it triggered Vang to return fire with his semi-automatic rifle.

The results were catastrophic. Within a few minutes, Vang had shot and killed six people: Robert Crotteau, Joseph Crotteau, Alan Laski, Mark Roidt, Jessica Willers, and Dennis Drew. Two others, Lauren Hesebeck and Terry Willers, were seriously wounded but survived. The violence was shocking in its speed and severity, transforming a typical hunting day into a scene of horror.

The Aftermath

Following the shootings, Chai Vang fled the scene but was apprehended by law enforcement later that day. The investigation revealed the scale of the tragedy and led to Vang's arrest and subsequent trial. The incident sparked widespread media coverage and public debate, with intense scrutiny on issues such as property rights, cultural differences, and gun control.

Vang's trial began in September 2005. His defense argued that he had acted in self-defense, claiming that he had been threatened and that racial slurs had been used against him. The prosecution, however, presented a case that depicted Vang as the aggressor who overreacted to a confrontation and used deadly force unnecessarily.

During the trial, Vang testified in his own defense, providing his account of the events. He claimed that he felt trapped and feared for his life when Willers allegedly fired the first shot. The prosecution countered with evidence and testimonies from the survivors and other witnesses, painting a picture of a deliberate and calculated attack by Vang.

On September 16, 2005, Chai Vang was found guilty of six counts of first-degree intentional homicide and three counts of attempted homicide. He was sentenced to six consecutive life terms in prison without the possibility of parole, plus an additional seventy years for attempted homicides.

Cultural and Social Implications

The Chai Vang case highlighted several important issues within the broader context of American society. One of the most significant was the cultural clash between the Hmong community and other rural, predominantly white communities in the Midwest. The Hmong tradition of hunting on public lands sometimes led to misunderstandings and conflicts over property boundaries and hunting rights.

Additionally, the case underscored the role of racial tensions in such conflicts. Vang's claim that racial slurs were used against him, though disputed, pointed to underlying prejudices and stereotypes that can exacerbate already volatile situations. This aspect of the case drew attention to the need for greater cultural sensitivity and understanding between different communities.

The incident also spurred discussions about gun control and the use of firearms. The rapid escalation of the confrontation into a deadly shootout highlighted the potential for violence when guns are present, and emotions run high. This aspect of the case contributed to ongoing debates about gun laws and the regulation of hunting practices.

Legacy

The Chai Vang murders left a lasting impact on the families of the victims, the survivors, and the wider community. The loss of life was a devastating blow, and the traumatic nature of the event scared those who were directly involved. For the Hmong community, the incident was a painful reminder of the challenges they faced in integrating into American society while preserving their cultural traditions.

In the years since the shootings, efforts have been made to improve relations between the Hmong community and other residents of rural areas in Wisconsin and Minnesota. Educational initiatives and community outreach programs aim to foster better understanding and cooperation, reducing the likelihood of such tragedies in the future.

Chai Vang's story remains a cautionary tale about the dangers of cultural misunderstandings and the potential for violence in confrontational situations. It serves as a reminder of the importance of empathy, communication, and respect for diverse traditions and perspectives. The lessons learned from this tragic incident continue to resonate, offering insights into the complexities of multiculturalism and the need for harmonious coexistence in an increasingly diverse society.

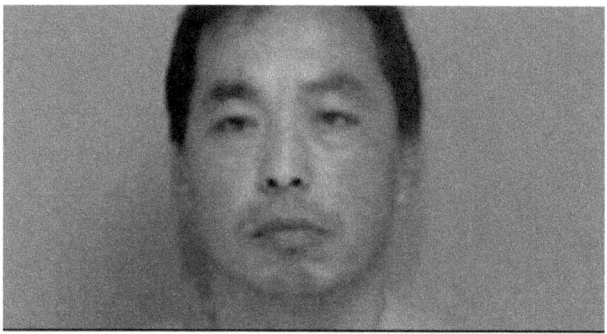

Chai Vang

Chapter 12

Radcliffe Haughton

Radcliffe Haughton was a name that became synonymous with tragedy and domestic violence in Wisconsin in October 2012. His actions culminated in a horrifying mass shooting at the Azana Salon & Spa in Brookfield, Wisconsin, leaving three women dead and four others injured. The incident, which ultimately ended in Haughton's suicide, drew national attention to the issues of domestic abuse, gun control, and the response of law enforcement to threats of violence.

Early Life and Background

Radcliffe Franklin Haughton, born on May 20, 1967, in the Virgin Islands, later moved to the United States, where he settled in Wisconsin. Little is known about his early life and background, but what is clear is that his life would take a dark and tragic turn. Haughton was a former Marine, and at the time of the shooting, he was working as a car salesman.

Haughton married Zina Daniel, and the couple had a daughter together. However, their relationship was fraught with issues, primarily revolving around Haughton's increasingly violent and controlling behavior. Over the years, Zina Haughton experienced escalating abuse and threats from her husband, culminating in her seeking legal protection.

Escalation of Domestic Violence

The warning signs of Haughton's violent tendencies were evident long before the tragic events at Azana Salon & Spa. In January 2011, police were called to the Haughton residence due to a domestic disturbance. During this incident, Zina reported that Haughton had thrown her clothing around the house and had physically intimidated her. Although no charges were filed, it was a clear indicator of the turmoil within the Haughton household.

The situation escalated dramatically in the months leading up to the shooting. In October 2012, Zina Haughton obtained a restraining order against her husband after an incident in which he slashed her car's tires. The restraining order was granted on October 8, just two weeks before the shooting, and it prohibited Haughton from contacting his wife or going near her workplace.

The Azana Salon & Spa Shooting

Despite the restraining order, Radcliffe Haughton was determined to confront his wife. On October 21, 2012, he arrived at the Azana Salon & Spa in Brookfield, where Zina worked as a hairstylist. Armed with a .40-caliber semi-automatic handgun, Haughton stormed into the salon, intent on finding and killing his wife.

The details of what transpired inside the salon are harrowing. Haughton opened fire indiscriminately, killing three women and wounding four others. Among the deceased was Zina Haughton, his primary target. The other victims were salon employees and clients who were tragically caught in the crossfire.

Amidst the chaos, survivors and witnesses recounted scenes of terror as they tried to escape or hide from the gunman. Some fled through the back doors, while others barricaded themselves in treatment rooms, desperately calling for help. The rapid response from law enforcement helped to secure the scene and evacuate those who were trapped inside.

The Aftermath

After the shooting, Haughton retreated to an upper level of the salon, where he took his own life. His death brought an end to the immediate threat, but the impact of his actions resonated far beyond the walls of the Azana Salon & Spa. The community of Brookfield, and indeed the entire state of Wisconsin, was left reeling from the senseless violence.

The investigation that followed revealed the extent of Haughton's premeditation. He had purchased the handgun used in the shooting just days before the attack, exploiting a loophole in gun laws that allowed him to bypass the waiting period for firearm purchases. This raised significant concerns and debates about gun control and the effectiveness of restraining orders in preventing domestic violence.

Lessons and Reforms

The tragedy of Radcliffe Haughton and the Azana Salon & Spa shooting highlighted several critical issues. Firstly, it underscored the severe consequences of domestic violence and the need for more effective intervention and support systems for victims. Zina Haughton's attempts to protect herself through legal means were ultimately insufficient to prevent the deadly outcome.

Secondly, the incident exposed gaps in gun control legislation, particularly concerning individuals with a history of domestic violence. The ease with which Haughton acquired a firearm despite the restraining order prompted calls for stricter background checks and closing of loopholes that allow abusers to access weapons.

In response to the shooting, Wisconsin lawmakers and advocacy groups pushed for reforms. Measures to strengthen restraining orders, improve the tracking and enforcement of firearms restrictions for domestic abusers, and enhance support services for victims were all part of the discussions that followed. The incident also spurred community efforts to raise awareness about domestic violence and promote resources available to those in need.

Memorials and Healing

The memory of the victims of the Azana Salon & Spa shooting continues to be honored by the community. Memorials and vigils were held in the aftermath of the tragedy, providing a space for collective mourning and reflection. The salon itself reopened after renovations, serving as a symbol of resilience and recovery.

For the families of the victims, the pain of their loss remains a constant reality. The lives of Zina Haughton, Cary L. Robuck, and Maelin Lind were cut short by senseless violence, leaving behind loved ones who continue to grapple with their absence. Their stories are a poignant reminder of the human toll of domestic violence and the urgent need for continued efforts to prevent such tragedies.

Conclusion

The story of Radcliffe Haughton and the Azana Salon & Spa shooting is a somber chapter in Wisconsin's history. It serves as a stark reminder of the dangers posed by domestic violence and the critical importance of effective legal protections and support systems for victims. The tragedy also highlights the ongoing challenges in gun control legislation and the need for comprehensive reforms to prevent abusers from obtaining firearms.

As the community of Brookfield and the wider public continue to heal from the events of October 21, 2012, the lessons learned from this incident remain relevant. It is a call to action for policymakers, law enforcement, and society at large to work towards a future where such senseless acts of violence are prevented, and victims of domestic abuse are provided with the protection and support they need.

Radcliffe Haughton

Chapter 13

Laurie "Bambi" Bembenek

Laurie "Bambi" Bembenek's story is one of intrigue, controversy, and dramatic courtroom battles that captivated the public and media for decades. Bembenek, an American former police officer and convicted murderer, became widely known for her high-profile case, which involved allegations of wrongful conviction, sensational trial coverage, and a series of legal and personal battles that spanned many years. Her story touches on themes of justice, media influence, and the complexity of the American legal system.

Early Life and Background

Laurie Bembenek was born on August 15, 1958, in the working-class neighborhood of Milwaukee, Wisconsin. Raised in a turbulent environment, her early years were marked by struggles, including her parents' divorce and a series of personal challenges. Despite these difficulties, Bembenek managed to pursue a career in law enforcement, joining the Milwaukee Police Department (MPD) as a police officer.

Her time with the MPD, however, was fraught with personal and professional challenges. Bembenek's interactions with colleagues and her handling of various police duties were characterized by a mix of dedication and controversy. She married and later divorced a fellow police officer, and her personal life became increasingly entangled with her professional responsibilities.

The Crime and Conviction

The events that would later make Bembenek a household name began on the night of May 28, 1981. On that evening, Christine Rudy, the wife of Bembenek's former boss, was found murdered in her Milwaukee home. Christine had been shot twice in the head, and the crime scene suggested a brutal and personal attack.

The investigation quickly focused on Bembenek, who had been having an affair with Rudy's husband, a wealthy and influential man named Daniel Rudy. The affair, coupled with Bembenek's troubled personal life and a series of circumstantial evidence, led to her arrest and subsequent conviction for the murder of Christine Rudy.

Bembenek's trial was a media sensation, with sensationalized coverage that painted her as a femme fatale caught in a web of scandal and betrayal. The prosecution argued that Bembenek, driven by jealousy and anger, had committed the crime. They presented evidence that included testimony from witnesses who claimed to have seen Bembenek in the vicinity of the crime scene and forensic evidence that appeared to link her to the murder.

The defense, led by attorney Charles J. G. "Charlie" Gessner, argued that Bembenek had been framed and that the evidence against her was circumstantial and unreliable. Despite their efforts, Bembenek was convicted of first-degree murder in 1982 and sentenced to life imprisonment without the possibility of parole.

The Media Circus

Bembenek's trial attracted significant media attention, and the coverage was often sensational and biased. The media portrayed her as a "bimbo," using derogatory terms and focusing on her physical appearance and personal life rather than the facts of the case. The portrayal of Bembenek as a high-profile criminal amplified the public's fascination with her story, leading to widespread media scrutiny and sensationalism.

The media coverage played a significant role in shaping public perception of the case, often overshadowing the legal and factual aspects of the trial. This focus on sensationalism rather than substantive legal arguments contributed to the complexity and controversy surrounding Bembenek's conviction.

The Fight for Justice

From the moment she was convicted, Laurie Bembenek maintained her innocence and fought tirelessly to overturn her conviction. Her case became a cause célèbre, with many advocates and supporters rallying behind her. Bembenek's supporters included legal experts, journalists, and celebrities who believed in her innocence and criticized the flaws in the judicial process that led to her conviction.

Bembenek's legal team pursued multiple avenues for appeal, arguing that there were significant errors and injustices in her trial. They highlighted issues such as the alleged mishandling of evidence, the potential for judicial bias, and the questionable credibility of key witnesses. Despite their efforts, Bembenek's appeals were largely unsuccessful, and her conviction remained in place.

One of the most significant developments in Bembenek's case came in 1990 when her legal team discovered new evidence that suggested a possible alternative suspect. The evidence pointed to a man named Michael J. Richards, who had a history of violent behavior and was known to have been in the vicinity of the crime scene. This new evidence raised questions about Bembenek's guilt and prompted renewed calls for a reinvestigation of the case.

The Escape and Capture

In 1990, Bembenek made headlines again when she managed to escape from prison. Using a combination of cunning and determination, Bembenek planned and executed her escape from the Milwaukee County Jail. She had been serving her sentence at the Wisconsin Correctional Institution, but her escape from jail led to a nationwide manhunt.

Bembenek's escape was highly publicized, and she became a fugitive. Her escape further fueled media coverage and public interest in her case. Despite the extensive search efforts, Bembenek was eventually recaptured in Canada after several months on the run. She was returned to the United States and faced additional legal consequences for her escape.

The Exoneration and Release

Bembenek's case continued to evolve over the years, and in 1992, she was granted a new trial based on the new evidence that had emerged. The new trial offered hope for her supporters and advocates, who believed that Bembenek's conviction could be overturned.

However, the legal process was lengthy and complex. Despite the new evidence and ongoing efforts by her legal team, Bembenek's attempts to secure her release were met with numerous legal and procedural challenges. The case remained in the public eye, and Bembenek's supporters continued to advocate for her innocence and push for justice.

In 1998, Laurie Bembenek's legal team reached a settlement with the state of Wisconsin, resulting in her release from prison. Although she was not formally exonerated, the settlement allowed her to leave prison and live outside of incarceration. Her release was met with mixed reactions, with some viewing it as a victory for justice and others as a controversial and unresolved chapter in her case.

Life After Prison

Following her release, Bembenek's life continued to be marked by public scrutiny and legal battles. She struggled to reintegrate into society and faced challenges related to her past conviction and the media attention surrounding her case.

Bembenek lived a relatively quiet life after her release, but her story remained a topic of interest for those following high-profile criminal cases and wrongful convictions. Her case continued to be cited as an example of the complexities and challenges associated with the American legal system, media influence, and the quest for justice.

In 2010, Laurie Bembenek passed away from cancer at the age of 52. Her death marked the end of a tumultuous and highly publicized chapter in her life. The legacy of her case continues to be a subject of discussion and analysis, reflecting on the broader issues of wrongful convictions, media influence, and the pursuit of justice.

Legacy and Impact

Laurie "Bambi" Bembenek's story is a reminder of the complexities and challenges of the American legal system. Her case highlighted issues related to wrongful convictions, media influence, and the difficulties faced by individuals navigating the criminal justice system. Bembenek's story continues to be studied and analyzed as a significant example of the intersection of law, media, and public perception.

The case also prompted discussions about the need for reforms in the legal system, including improvements in the handling of evidence, the treatment of defendants, and the influence of media coverage on high-profile cases. Bembenek's case remains a poignant reminder of the importance of ensuring that justice is served and that the rights of individuals are protected throughout the legal process.

In summary, Laurie "Bambi" Bembenek's story is one of intrigue, controversy, and dramatic courtroom battles. Her case captivated the public and media, highlighting the complexities of the American legal system and the impact of media influence on high-profile trials. Bembenek's life and legal battles remain a subject of interest and discussion, reflecting broader issues related to justice, media, and the pursuit of truth.

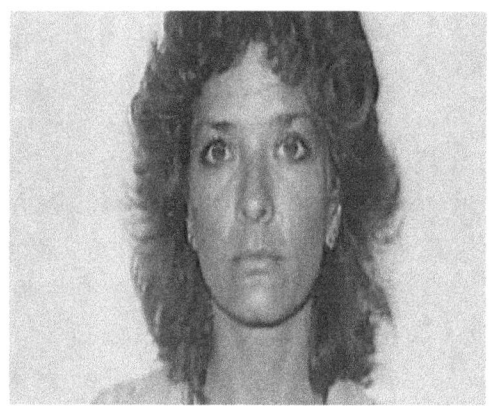

Laurie Bembenek

Chapter 14

Edward Wayne Edwards

Edward Wayne Edwards is a name that resonates ominously in the annals of American criminal history. A notorious serial killer, Edwards led a life of deception, eluding law enforcement for decades before his eventual capture and conviction. Born in Akron, Ohio, in 1933, Edwards's life was marred by crime and violence from an early age, ultimately leading to a series of brutal murders that spanned several states, including Wisconsin.

Edwards's criminal career began with a series of petty crimes. He was frequently in trouble with the law and spent a significant portion of his early years in juvenile detention and later in prison. His criminal activities ranged from theft and armed robbery to assault. However, it was his ability to manipulate and deceive that made him particularly dangerous. Edwards often used his charm to gain the trust of those around him, only to betray them later in the most heinous ways.

The first known murders committed by Edwards occurred in 1977, when he brutally killed a young couple, Billy Lavaco and Judy Straub, in Ohio. The couple was shot in the neck and head while they were parked in a secluded area. The crime remained unsolved for years, with Edwards managing to avoid detection by moving frequently and changing his identity.

It wasn't until the murder of another couple, Tim Hack and Kelly Drew, in Wisconsin in 1980 that Edwards began to leave a more discernible trail. Hack and Drew disappeared after attending a wedding reception at the Concord House in Sullivan, Wisconsin. Their bodies were found weeks later in a wooded area, showing signs of torture and strangulation. The brutality of the crime shocked the small community and prompted an intensive investigation. However, despite the efforts of law enforcement, the case went cold for nearly three decades.

Edwards continued his killing spree, moving across states and leaving a trail of bodies in his wake. In 1996, he murdered his foster son, Danny Boy Edwards, in Burton, Ohio. This murder was staged to look like suicide, but Edwards's motive was financial gain, as he hoped to collect on a life insurance policy. This act of cold-blooded calculation showcased his cunning nature and willingness to exploit anyone, even his own family, for his benefit.

The breakthrough in the case came in 2009 when advancements in DNA technology allowed investigators to revisit the unsolved murders. DNA evidence linked Edwards to the murder of Tim Hack and Kelly Drew, finally providing the crucial piece of evidence needed to apprehend him. Edwards was arrested at his home in Louisville, Kentucky, and subsequently confessed to the murders of Hack and Drew, as well as the murders of Billy Lavaco and Judy Straub.

During his trial, Edwards displayed a chilling lack of remorse. His confessions were detailed and graphic, revealing a deep-seated enjoyment of the pain and suffering he inflicted on his victims. The courtroom was filled with a sense of disbelief and horror as Edwards recounted his crimes with a disturbingly casual demeanor.

In 2010, Edwards was sentenced to life in prison without the possibility of parole for the murders of Hack and Drew. However, his story didn't end there. Edwards continued to make headlines by confessing to additional murders, some of which had remained unsolved for decades. His confessions led to the reopening of several cold cases, as investigators sought to uncover the full extent of his murderous activities.

One of the most controversial aspects of Edwards's case is the theory that he may have been responsible for several other high-profile murders, including the infamous Zodiac killings. Some researchers and amateur sleuths believe that Edwards's pattern of movement and the nature of his crimes bear similarities to those of the Zodiac Killer. While these theories remain speculative and unproven, they add a layer of intrigue to an already horrifying story.

Edwards's life and crimes serve as a stark reminder of the dark potential within human nature. His ability to evade capture for so long, coupled with his apparent lack of conscience, make him one of the most chilling figures in American criminal history. His case also highlights the importance of advancements in forensic science, which ultimately played a crucial role in bringing him to justice.

The legacy of Edward Wayne Edwards is one of fear and tragedy. His victims, whose lives were cut short by his brutal actions, are remembered as innocent souls who fell prey to a master manipulator. Their stories are a poignant reminder of the fragility of life and the enduring impact of violence on communities.

In Wisconsin, the murders of Tim Hack and Kelly Drew remain etched in the collective memory of the community. The once-cold case that haunted the small town for nearly 30 years finally saw justice, thanks to the persistence of law enforcement and the power of modern technology. Edwards's capture and conviction brought a sense of closure to the families of his victims, but the scars left by his actions continue to linger.

As we reflect on the life and crimes of Edward Wayne Edwards, it is crucial to remember the importance of vigilance and the pursuit of justice. While his story is one of darkness and depravity, it also serves as a testament to the resilience of those who seek to uncover the truth and bring perpetrators to account. The case of Edward Wayne Edwards is a haunting chapter in the history of American crime, a reminder of the evil that can lurk behind a seemingly ordinary facade.

Edward Edwards

Chapter 15

Richard Otto Macek

Early Life and Criminal Beginnings

Richard Otto Macek was born on October 7, 1938, in Lake County, Illinois. His early life was marked by instability and criminal behavior. He was in and out of juvenile detention centers and developed a criminal record that included burglary and theft. Macek's violent tendencies became more pronounced as he grew older, eventually leading him down a path of brutal assaults and murders.

By the 1970s, Macek's criminal activities had escalated significantly. He had become adept at evading law enforcement, often moving from state to state to avoid capture. His criminal record extended across Illinois, Indiana, and Wisconsin, making him a challenging target for police.

The Crimes

Macek's most infamous crime spree began in the early 1970s, targeting women in Illinois and Wisconsin. His modus operandi was particularly gruesome: he would break into homes, assault his victims, and then bite them savagely, leaving deep, identifiable bite marks. This unique signature eventually earned him the nickname "Mad Biter."

One of Macek's earliest known victims was Janet Raas, a 19-year-old woman from Harvard, Illinois. On October 2, 1973, Janet was found brutally murdered in her home. She had been sexually assaulted and bitten multiple times. The horrific nature of the crime shocked the local community and left law enforcement scrambling for leads. Despite their efforts, the case remained unsolved for several years.

The Wisconsin Connection

Macek's crimes continued unabated, and he soon turned his attention to Wisconsin. In 1974, he committed one of his most notorious murders in the small town of McFarland, Wisconsin. On the night of August 8, 1974, he broke into the home of Mary Kay Schmal, a 24-year-old woman who was home alone. Macek assaulted Mary Kay, strangled her, and left her lifeless body on the floor. Her husband discovered her body when he returned home from work, and the bite marks on her body were a clear indication that the "Mad Biter" had struck again.

The murder of Mary Kay Schmal sent shockwaves through the quiet town of McFarland. Local law enforcement, along with the Wisconsin Division of Criminal Investigation, launched an intensive investigation. However, Macek's ability to evade capture and his transient lifestyle made it difficult for authorities to track him down.

Capture and Trial

Macek's downfall began in 1975 when he was arrested in Indiana for an unrelated burglary charge.

During his incarceration, investigators began to connect the dots between Macek and the string of unsolved murders in Illinois and Wisconsin. The distinctive bite marks left on his victims were a crucial piece of evidence that linked him to the crimes.

In 1977, Macek was extradited to Wisconsin to stand trial for the murder of Mary Kay Schmal. The prosecution's case was bolstered by forensic evidence, including the bite marks that matched Macek's dental impressions. Additionally, witnesses testified about Macek's violent tendencies and his presence in the areas where the murders had occurred.

The trial was a media sensation, with graphic details of Macek's crimes making headlines. The prosecution painted a picture of a sadistic killer who took pleasure in inflicting pain and suffering on his victims. Macek's defense, on the other hand, attempted to cast doubt on the forensic evidence and the reliability of witness testimonies.

Despite the defense's efforts, the overwhelming evidence against Macek led to his conviction. In 1978, he was found guilty of the murder of Mary Kay Schmal and was sentenced to life in prison without the possibility of parole. The verdict brought a sense of relief to the communities affected by Macek's reign of terror, but the scars left by his crimes remained.

Impact and Legacy

The case of Richard Otto Macek had a profound impact on forensic science and law enforcement practices. The use of bite mark analysis in his trial was a significant development in forensic dentistry, highlighting the importance of dental evidence in criminal investigations. This case set a precedent for the use of forensic odontology in solving crimes, paving the way for its widespread adoption in future cases.

Macek's crimes also underscored the importance of interstate collaboration among law enforcement agencies. His ability to evade capture by moving between states highlighted the need for better communication and coordination among police departments. The establishment of the Violent Criminal Apprehension Program (ViCAP) in 1985 was, in part, a response to cases like Macek's, aiming to facilitate the sharing of information and resources to track and apprehend serial offenders.

The Victims

While the story of Richard Otto Macek is one of brutal violence and criminal cunning, it is essential to remember the victims whose lives were tragically cut short by his actions. Janet Raas and Mary Kay

Schmal were vibrant young women with bright futures ahead of them. Their murders left a lasting impact on their families and communities, who continue to mourn their loss.

Janet Raas's family struggled for years with the unresolved nature of her murder. The eventual conviction of Macek provided some closure, but the pain of losing Janet in such a horrific manner remained a constant burden. Similarly, the Schmal family had to navigate the trauma of losing Mary Kay and the subsequent media attention that the trial brought.

Reflection

The case of Richard Otto Macek serves as a stark reminder of the capacity for human cruelty and the enduring impact of violent crime on victims and their families. It also highlights the critical role of forensic science in the pursuit of justice. The advancements in forensic odontology and the lessons learned from Macek's case have contributed to the development of more sophisticated investigative techniques, improving the ability of law enforcement to solve crimes and bring perpetrators to justice.

Macek's story is a cautionary tale about the dangers of unchecked violent behavior and the importance of vigilance in protecting our communities. His capture and conviction were the result of relentless dedication and collaboration among law enforcement professionals, who worked tirelessly to ensure that justice was served.

Conclusion

Richard Otto Macek's reign of terror left an indelible mark on the communities he targeted and the families of his victims. His brutal crimes and distinctive modus operandi earned him the moniker "Mad Biter" and a place in the annals of American criminal history. The advancements in forensic science and law enforcement practices that emerged from his case continue to benefit the pursuit of justice today.

While Macek will forever be remembered as a sadistic killer, it is crucial to honor the memory of his victims and the resilience of their families. The story of Richard Otto Macek is not just one of horror and brutality but also of the enduring quest for justice and the importance of never forgetting those who suffered at the hands of a violent predator.

Chapter 16

Tyler Peterson

Tyler Peterson, a name that reverberates with shock and sorrow in the small town of Crandon, Wisconsin, became infamously known for the tragic events of October 7, 2007. As a 20-year-old off-duty sheriff's deputy, Peterson's actions on that fateful night left an indelible mark on the community, resulting in a massacre that claimed the lives of six young individuals and forever altered the lives of many others. This tragedy, often referred to as the "Crandon Shooting," remains a poignant reminder of the potential for violence to erupt from unexpected quarters and the profound impact such events have on small, tight-knit communities.

The Background of Tyler Peterson

Tyler Peterson was born and raised in Crandon, a town with a population of just over 2,000 people. Known to many in the community, he was generally seen as a typical young man. Peterson graduated from Crandon High School and later attended Nicolet Area Technical College. He pursued a career in law enforcement, joining the Forest County Sheriff's Department, where he was known for his work ethic and commitment. However, underneath this seemingly normal exterior, Peterson harbored deep-seated issues that would tragically manifest in the most horrific way.

The Night of the Shooting

The evening of October 6, 2007, began like any other Saturday night for a group of friends who gathered at a house party in Crandon. Among them was Tyler Peterson, who was off duty at the time. The party, attended by young adults and teenagers, including some of Peterson's former high school classmates, was supposed to be a night of fun and relaxation. However, as the night wore on, tensions began to rise.

Reports suggest that Peterson became increasingly agitated and was involved in a confrontation with his ex-girlfriend, Jordanne Murray, who was among the partygoers. The exact details of what transpired between Peterson and Murray remain unclear, but it is believed that a combination of personal issues, jealousy, and perhaps alcohol fueled Peterson's anger to a boiling point.

At around 2:45 a.m. on October 7, Peterson left the party, only to return shortly afterward with an AR-15 rifle. What followed was a scene of unimaginable horror. Peterson opened fire inside the house, systematically targeting the partygoers. In a matter of minutes, six people were dead, and one was critically injured. The victims, all young adults, included:

- **Jordanne Murray (18)**: Peterson's ex-girlfriend, who was believed to be a primary target.
- **Bradley Schultz (20)**: A close friend of many at the party.
- **Aaron Smith (20)**: Another friend and local resident.
- **Katrina McCorkle (18)**: A high school student and friend of the group.
- **Leah L. Michalak (18)**: Another friend and party attendee.
- **Rosie A. Lombardo (17)**: A younger member of the group, who tragically lost her life.

The sole survivor, 21-year-old Lindsay R. Siegler, sustained severe injuries but managed to escape the massacre. She was rushed to a hospital in nearby Marshfield, where she underwent multiple surgeries and began a long and painful recovery process.

The Aftermath and Manhunt

Following the shooting, Peterson fled the scene, setting off a massive manhunt involving local, state, and federal law enforcement agencies. The town of Crandon, gripped by fear and disbelief, was effectively locked down as authorities searched for Peterson. As news of the shooting spread, the small community was inundated with media coverage, with journalists and news crews descending on the town.

During the manhunt, Peterson made a series of phone calls to friends and family, expressing remorse for his actions and contemplating suicide. His mental state, already fragile, had deteriorated further in the wake of the massacre. After a tense standoff with the police, Peterson took his own life in the woods near Argonne, Wisconsin, bringing an end to the immediate threat but leaving behind a community shattered by his actions.

Community Impact and Reflection

The Crandon Shooting sent shockwaves through the small town and beyond. The scale of the tragedy was almost incomprehensible for a community where everyone knew each other. The loss of six young lives in such a brutal manner left an enduring scar on the town's collective consciousness.

In the days and weeks following the shooting, Crandon residents came together to mourn and support one another. Vigils, memorials, and community gatherings were held to honor the victims and provide solace to those affected. The local high school, where many of the victims had been students, became a focal point for grief and remembrance.

Examination of Law Enforcement Policies

The fact that Tyler Peterson was an off-duty sheriff's deputy raised significant questions about law enforcement policies and the screening processes for those in positions of authority. Peterson's actions highlighted the potential dangers of individuals with unresolved personal issues and access to firearms. In response to the tragedy, the Forest County Sheriff's Department, along with other law enforcement agencies, reviewed their hiring practices, mental health evaluations, and policies regarding firearm access for officers.

Mental Health Awareness

The Crandon Shooting also underscored the importance of mental health awareness and intervention. Peterson's descent into violence was a stark reminder of how untreated mental health issues can lead to catastrophic outcomes. The tragedy spurred discussions on the need for better mental health support and resources, both within law enforcement and the broader community. Efforts were made to increase awareness of mental health issues, reduce stigma, and provide more accessible support for those in need.

Legacy of the Victims

While the memory of the Crandon Shooting is undoubtedly a painful one, the legacy of the victims lives on through the actions and efforts of their families and the community. Scholarships and foundations were established in their names, aiming to provide educational opportunities and support for young people in the area. These initiatives serve as a testament to the enduring impact of the victims' lives and a commitment to fostering positive change in the aftermath of tragedy.

Conclusion

The Crandon Shooting, perpetrated by Tyler Peterson, remains one of Wisconsin's most heartbreaking and significant criminal events. It serves as a somber reminder of the potential for violence to emerge from unexpected sources and the devastating impact it can have on a community. As Crandon continues to heal and move forward, the memories of the victims and the lessons learned from this tragedy continue to shape efforts to prevent such events in the future. The resilience of the community, the importance of mental health awareness, and the need for vigilant law enforcement practices are enduring themes that emerge from this dark chapter in Wisconsin's history.

Tyler Peterson

Chapter 17

Christopher Scarver

Christopher Scarver is a name that many associate with one of the most infamous incidents in the American prison system. Known primarily for the murder of serial killer Jeffrey Dahmer and fellow inmate Jesse Anderson while incarcerated, Scarver's own story is a complex and troubling one, rooted in a life of hardship, mental illness, and a deep sense of justice that led to his notorious actions. This account delves into the life and crimes of Christopher Scarver, providing a comprehensive look at the events that shaped him and his impact on Wisconsin's criminal history.

Early Life and Background

Christopher Scarver was born on July 6, 1969, in Milwaukee, Wisconsin. Raised in a low-income family, Scarver faced numerous challenges from a young age. His childhood was marked by instability, with his family often struggling to make ends meet. Scarver dropped out of high school during his junior year, and his life began to spiral downward as he faced unemployment and the absence of stable familial support.

In the late 1980s, Scarver found work through a Wisconsin Conservation Corps job program, but his employment was short-lived. Fired from his job, Scarver began to experience severe mental health issues, including paranoid schizophrenia. These issues were compounded by substance abuse, further destabilizing his already fragile mental state.

The Murder of Steven Lohman

Scarver's descent into violence culminated on June 1, 1990, when he committed his first murder. After being fired from his job, Scarver returned to the Wisconsin Conservation Corps office, seeking retribution. Armed with a .25-caliber pistol, he confronted his former supervisor, John Feyen, and site manager, Steven Lohman, demanding money. When Lohman handed him a mere $15, Scarver, enraged by what he perceived as an insult, shot him in the head, killing him instantly. Feyen managed to escape and alert the authorities.

Following the murder, Scarver was apprehended and charged with first-degree murder. He was subsequently convicted and sentenced to life in prison without the possibility of parole. Scarver was sent to the Columbia Correctional Institution in Portage, Wisconsin, where he would later cross paths with two other notorious inmates.

Life in Prison and the Murder of Jeffrey Dahmer and Jesse Anderson

While serving his life sentence, Scarver continued to struggle with his mental health. His schizophrenia went largely untreated, and he became increasingly paranoid and delusional. By the early 1990s, Scarver was housed in the same prison as Jeffrey Dahmer, the notorious serial killer who had been convicted of murdering 17 young men and boys, and Jesse Anderson, who was serving a life sentence for the murder of his wife.

On the morning of November 28, 1994, Scarver, Dahmer, and Anderson were assigned to work together on a cleaning detail in the prison gym. Unsupervised by guards for a brief period, Scarver seized the opportunity to confront Dahmer and Anderson. Armed with a metal bar from the weight room, Scarver attacked Dahmer first, striking him repeatedly in the head. Dahmer succumbed to his injuries shortly thereafter. Scarver then turned his attention to Anderson, bludgeoning him as well. Anderson died from his injuries two days later.

Motives and Confessions

Scarver later explained his motives for the attacks during interviews and legal proceedings. He claimed that both Dahmer and Anderson had provoked him, and he expressed a deep sense of justice for Dahmer's heinous crimes. Scarver stated that he had been tormented by Dahmer's macabre sense of humor and his unsettling interactions with other inmates. According to Scarver, Dahmer would fashion his food into shapes resembling severed body parts, a macabre reminder of his gruesome crimes.

Scarver also believed that he was acting under divine guidance. He claimed that he had received messages from God instructing him to kill Dahmer and Anderson. This belief, coupled with his untreated mental illness, created a dangerous and volatile situation that ultimately led to the fatal confrontation.

Legal and Psychiatric Evaluations

Following the murders of Dahmer and Anderson, Scarver was charged with two counts of first-degree intentional homicide. His legal defense centered around his mental health issues, with his attorneys arguing that his actions were driven by his severe schizophrenia. Psychiatrists who evaluated Scarver confirmed his diagnosis, noting that his delusions and paranoia had significantly impaired his judgment.

Despite his mental health condition, Scarver was found guilty of the murders and received two additional life sentences, to be served consecutively with his existing life sentence. He was transferred to a federal prison and later moved to the Centennial Correctional Facility in Colorado, where he remains incarcerated.

Reflections on Justice and Morality

The case of Christopher Scarver raises complex questions about justice, morality, and the treatment of mental illness within the criminal justice system. Scarver's actions, while undeniably violent and criminal, were influenced by a combination of personal vendettas, mental illness, and a distorted sense of justice. His killing of Jeffrey Dahmer elicited mixed reactions from the public. Some saw Scarver as a vigilante who delivered justice to a notorious serial killer, while others viewed his actions as another tragic instance of violence begetting more violence.

Scarver himself has reflected on his actions with a sense of remorse and resignation. In interviews, he has acknowledged the pain and suffering he caused, expressing regret for the lives he took and the impact on the victims' families. His story serves as a stark reminder of the need for comprehensive mental health care within the prison system and the broader society, highlighting the potential consequences of neglecting those in need of psychological support.

Conclusion

Christopher Scarver's life and crimes are a testament to the complexities of human behavior, the impact of untreated mental illness, and the profound consequences of violence. His story is inextricably linked with that of Jeffrey Dahmer, one of America's most infamous serial killers, but it also stands on its own as a tragic tale of a man whose life was marked by hardship, mental illness, and ultimately, acts of extreme violence. As Scarver continues to serve his sentence, his case remains a poignant example of the intricate interplay between mental health, justice, and morality in the criminal justice system.

Christopher Scarver

Chapter 18

John McGaffary

Jon McGaffary is a lesser known but deeply disturbing figure in Wisconsin's criminal history. His case is emblematic of a profound personal tragedy that escalated into horrific violence, leaving a permanent scar on the community and the families involved. This narrative will delve into the background of McGaffary, the details of his crime, its aftermath, and its impact on the local community.

Early Life and Background

Jon McGaffary was born and raised in Wisconsin, in a seemingly typical American family. His early life did not hint at the violent path he would later take. Like many children growing up in the Midwest, he attended public schools, played sports, and had friends. However, beneath the surface, there were signs of trouble. McGaffary had a difficult relationship with his family, particularly his parents, which would later contribute to his emotional instability.

By his teenage years, McGaffary began to exhibit signs of psychological distress. He struggled with anger management issues, had frequent outbursts, and became increasingly isolated. Despite these warning signs, his behavior was often dismissed as typical teenage angst. His mental health continued to deteriorate, but he never received the comprehensive psychological care he needed. This lack of intervention would prove catastrophic.

The Crime

On the night of October 30, 1988, Jon McGaffary committed one of the most brutal murders in Wisconsin's recent history. Fueled by a combination of deep-seated rage and untreated mental illness, McGaffary snapped, leading to a horrifying chain of events. His victims were his own family members: his mother, father, and younger sister.

McGaffary's actions that night was both calculated and frenzied. Using a hunting knife, he first attacked his father in the living room, catching him off guard and inflicting multiple fatal stab wounds. The violence of the attack was staggering, and the scene was gruesome. Hearing the commotion, McGaffary's mother rushed into the room, only to meet the same fate. She fought back but was ultimately overpowered by her son. His younger sister, who was just twelve years old, became the final victim in his spree. Her death was particularly tragic, as she was innocent and defenseless.

The brutal nature of the crime shocked the local community. Neighbors, friends, and extended family members were left to grapple with the incomprehensible act of violence. The immediate aftermath was one of confusion, grief, and a desperate search for answers.

Investigation and Arrest

The investigation into the murders was swift. Police arrived at the scene shortly after McGaffary's sister managed to dial 911 during the attack. The house was a scene of horror, with evidence of a violent struggle and the bodies of the victims lying in pools of blood. McGaffary did not attempt to flee the scene; instead, he was found sitting in the kitchen, covered in blood and staring blankly ahead.

He was immediately taken into custody and charged with three counts of first-degree murder. During the interrogation, McGaffary's demeanor was detached and unresponsive. He offered no explanation for his actions, leaving investigators and the public to speculate about his motives.

The Trial

McGaffary's trial began in early 1989, and it quickly became a media spectacle. The prosecution painted him as a cold-blooded killer, driven by uncontrollable rage and resentment towards his family. They presented evidence of his troubled past, including testimonies from friends and acquaintances who described his erratic behavior and violent tendencies.

The defense, on the other hand, argued that McGaffary was not in control of his actions due to severe mental illness. They called upon expert witnesses who testified about his long history of psychological problems, including a diagnosis of paranoid schizophrenia. These experts argued that McGaffary's mental state had deteriorated to the point where he could no longer distinguish right from wrong.

The jury faced a difficult decision. On one hand, the brutality of the crime was undeniable. On the other, there was compelling evidence that McGaffary's actions were driven by severe mental illness. In the end, the jury found him guilty of three counts of first-degree murder but acknowledged his mental health issues. He was sentenced to life in prison without the possibility of parole, with a recommendation for psychiatric treatment.

Aftermath and Impact

The murders had a profound impact on the local community. The McGaffary family had been well-known and well-liked, and their violent deaths left a void that was felt by many. Neighbors and friends struggled to understand how such a tragedy could occur, and the community came together to mourn the loss of the three victims.

In the years following the crime, there was a renewed focus on mental health awareness and intervention in Wisconsin. The McGaffary case highlighted the importance of recognizing and addressing mental health issues before they escalate into violence. Local schools, healthcare providers, and community organizations began to implement more comprehensive mental health programs, aiming to prevent similar tragedies in the future.

Reflections on Justice and Mental Health

Jon McGaffary's case raises complex questions about justice, mental health, and societal responsibility. His actions were undeniably horrific, and he is rightly serving a life sentence for his crimes. However, his case also underscores the critical need for early intervention and treatment of mental health issues.

In many ways, McGaffary is a tragic figure. His life was marked by suffering and untreated psychological problems, which ultimately led him down a path of unimaginable violence. His story serves as a cautionary tale about the consequences of neglecting mental health and the importance of providing support and care to those in need.

Conclusion

The story of Jon McGaffary is a dark chapter in Wisconsin's history. It is a tale of a young man who, driven by untreated mental illness and deep-seated anger, committed an act of unimaginable violence against his own family. His case serves as a stark reminder of the importance of mental health awareness and the need for early intervention to prevent similar tragedies in the future.

As McGaffary serves out his life sentence, the community he left behind continues to grapple with the impact of his actions. The memories of his victims remain vivid, and the pain of their loss is felt by all who knew them. Through increased awareness and better mental health resources, there is hope that such a tragedy can be prevented from happening again, ensuring that the lessons learned from the McGaffary case are not forgotten.

Chapter 19

Terry Ratzmann

Terry Ratzmann was the perpetrator of a tragic mass shooting that took place on March 12, 2005, in Brookfield, Wisconsin. This incident, which shocked the local community and the nation, occurred at a Living Church of God service at the Sheraton Hotel. Ratzmann's actions left seven people dead, including himself, and four others injured. This narrative delves into the life of Terry Ratzmann, the events leading up to the shooting, the details of the crime itself, and the aftermath and implications for the community and beyond.

Early Life and Background

Terry Ratzmann was born on February 29, 1960, in New Berlin, Wisconsin. He grew up in a suburban neighborhood and was known to be a quiet and unassuming individual. He had a keen interest in computers and gardening, often spending his free time tending to his plants and working on his computer. Ratzmann lived with his mother and sister in a modest home, maintaining a relatively low-profile lifestyle.

Ratzmann was a devout member of the Living Church of God, a Christian denomination that adheres to strict biblical interpretations and practices. The church played a significant role in his life, providing him with a sense of community and belonging. However, despite his outwardly calm demeanor, those close to him noted that he had struggled with depression and feelings of isolation. He had lost his job as a computer technician a few months before the shooting, which further exacerbated his emotional instability.

The Events Leading Up to the Shooting

In the weeks and days leading up to the shooting, there were signs that Ratzmann was experiencing increasing distress. Friends and fellow church members reported that he seemed more withdrawn and agitated than usual. On the day of the shooting, Ratzmann attended a church service at the Sheraton Hotel in Brookfield, Wisconsin, as he had done many times before. However, this time, he carried with him a 9mm Glock 17 pistol.

It is believed that Ratzmann's actions were precipitated by a sermon he had heard two weeks earlier, which reportedly upset him deeply. He was also facing significant personal issues, including ongoing struggles with depression and unemployment. These factors, combined with his rigid religious beliefs and sense of alienation, created a volatile situation.

The Shooting

On March 12, 2005, during the Sabbath service, Terry Ratzmann opened fire on the congregation of the Living Church of God. The service was being held in a meeting room at the Sheraton Hotel, where approximately 50 members of the church were gathered. Without warning, Ratzmann stood up, pulled out his Glock 17, and began shooting indiscriminately.

The first shots were fired at the church pastor, Randy Gregory, and his family, who were sitting at the front of the room. Gregory's teenage son, James, was one of the first victims. Ratzmann then continued to fire at other members of the congregation, creating chaos and panic. Some people tried to flee the room, while others attempted to shield themselves behind chairs and tables.

The entire incident lasted only a few minutes but resulted in devastating consequences. Ratzmann killed seven people, including the pastor's son, James Gregory; Bart Oliver, another teenager; Richard Reeves; Harold Diekmeier; Gloria Critari; and Gerald and Wendy Miller. Four others were injured but survived the attack. After exhausting his ammunition, Ratzmann turned the gun on himself, committing suicide at the scene.

Immediate Aftermath

The immediate aftermath of the shooting was one of shock and disbelief. Emergency responders arrived quickly, but for many victims, it was already too late. The surviving members of the congregation were left to grapple with the horror of what had just occurred. The hotel was cordoned off as a crime scene, and investigators began the grim task of piecing together the events that led to the tragedy.

The news of the shooting spread rapidly, capturing national attention. The media descended upon Brookfield, seeking to understand the motives behind Ratzmann's actions. The small, tight-knit community was thrust into the spotlight, as friends, neighbors, and church members struggled to come to terms with the loss and devastation.

Investigative Findings

As investigators delved into Ratzmann's background, a clearer picture began to emerge. It became evident that he had been dealing with significant personal and psychological issues. His recent job loss, coupled with his deep religious convictions and feelings of isolation, seemed to have created a perfect storm that culminated in the mass shooting.

Investigators found no evidence that Ratzmann had planned the attack far in advance. Instead, it appeared to be a spontaneous act driven by a sudden emotional breakdown. The sermon that had upset him two weeks earlier was scrutinized, but it was determined that there was no specific message or incident that directly triggered the violence.

Community Impact

The impact of the shooting on the Brookfield community was profound and lasting. The Living Church of God congregation was devastated by the loss of so many members. The survivors faced a long and difficult road to recovery, both physically and emotionally. The church, which had been a source of comfort and community, now became a painful reminder of the tragedy.

In the broader community, the shooting prompted discussions about mental health, gun control, and the need for better support systems for individuals struggling with psychological issues. There was a recognition that more needed to be done to identify and help those at risk of committing violent acts.

Broader Implications and Lessons Learned

The Terry Ratzmann shooting underscored the complexities of addressing mental health issues in society. It highlighted the importance of early intervention and the need for accessible mental health care. Friends and family members of Ratzmann later expressed regret that they had not recognized the severity of his issues sooner and sought help from him.

The tragedy also sparked debates about gun control. The fact that Ratzmann was able to legally purchase and carry a firearm despite his known mental health issues raised questions about the adequacy of background checks and gun laws. Advocates for stricter gun control measures argued that better regulations could help prevent similar tragedies in the future.

In the wake of the shooting, there was an outpouring of support for the victims and their families. Vigils, memorials, and fundraisers were organized to help those affected by the tragedy. The community came together to mourn, heal, and support one another through the difficult times.

Reflections on Tragedy and Healing

The story of Terry Ratzmann and the Brookfield shooting is a sobering reminder of the potential for violence that can arise from untreated mental health issues and personal despair. It is a tragedy that left a deep scar on the community, but it also served as a catalyst for important conversations about mental health, gun control, and community support.

For the families of the victims, the pain of their loss is a daily reality. The memories of their loved ones, taken so suddenly and violently, are cherished and honored through various means, including memorials and community events. The survivors continue to rebuild their lives, carrying the burden of their experiences with them.

As time passes, the lessons learned from this tragedy remain relevant. The importance of recognizing and addressing mental health issues cannot be overstated. Communities must strive to create environments where individuals feel supported and where there are resources available for those in need. By doing so, we can hope to prevent future tragedies and ensure that those who are struggling receive the help and care they deserve.

Conclusion

The mass shooting perpetrated by Terry Ratzmann in 2005 is a tragic chapter in Wisconsin's history. It is a story of a man whose personal struggles and untreated mental health issues led to an act of unimaginable violence. The aftermath of the shooting left a community in mourning and prompted important discussions about mental health, gun control, and community support.

As we reflect on this tragedy, it is crucial to remember the victims and their families, and to honor their memories by working towards a society where such acts of violence are less likely to occur. Through increased awareness, better mental health resources, and stronger community support systems, we can strive to create a safer and more compassionate world for all.

Terry Ratzmann

Chapter 20

Jesse Anderson

Jesse Anderson's name is etched into Wisconsin's history due to a shocking and brutal crime that stunned the state and garnered nationwide attention. On April 21, 1992, Anderson stabbed his wife, Barbara Anderson, multiple times in the parking lot of a T.G.I. Friday's restaurant in Milwaukee, Wisconsin. The case became infamous not only because of the brutal nature of the crime but also due to Anderson's subsequent actions and the widespread media coverage that followed. This narrative delves into the life of Jesse Anderson, the events leading up to the murder, the details of the crime, and the aftermath, including his trial, conviction, and eventual death.

Early Life and Background

Jesse Anderson was born on May 3, 1957, in Alton, Illinois. He grew up in a seemingly normal middle-class family and later attended Elmhurst College in Illinois, where he earned a degree in business. After college, Anderson married Barbara, and the couple eventually moved to Cedarburg, Wisconsin. They had three children and appeared to lead a typical suburban life. Jesse worked in marketing and sales, while Barbara was a homemaker.

Despite the outward appearance of a stable and happy family, there were underlying issues. Jesse was known to have a controlling and manipulative personality, which created tension in the marriage. Friends and neighbors would later recall that the couple often argued, and there were signs of domestic trouble. However, no one anticipated the tragic turn their lives would take.

The Murder of Barbara Anderson

On the evening of April 21, 1992, Jesse and Barbara Anderson went to the T.G.I. Friday's restaurant on the north side of Milwaukee. After finishing their meal, they walked to their car in the restaurant's parking lot. It was there that Jesse attacked Barbara, stabbing her multiple times in the face, head, and torso. He then inflicted minor stab wounds on himself to make it appear as though they had been attacked by someone else.

In a desperate attempt to divert suspicion, Jesse concocted a story, claiming that they had been assaulted by two black men who had approached them in the parking lot. He described one of the supposed attackers as wearing a Los Angeles Clippers hat, which he had conveniently planted at the scene. This fabricated narrative was intended to exploit racial tensions and divert attention away from himself.

Barbara Anderson was rushed to the hospital but succumbed to her injuries two days later. Jesse's injuries were superficial, and he was released from the hospital shortly after being treated. The police initially pursued his version of events, but inconsistencies in his story and evidence at the crime scene quickly raised suspicions.

Investigation and Arrest

As the investigation progressed, several key pieces of evidence began to unravel Jesse's story. First, the wounds on Jesse were determined to be self-inflicted and inconsistent with a struggle. Additionally, the Los Angeles Clippers hat found at the scene was traced back to a purchase Jesse had made just days before the attack. Witnesses also reported seeing no other individuals in the parking lot at the time of the incident, further discrediting Jesse's account.

Moreover, Jesse had purchased a knife like the one used in the attack shortly before the murder, and blood evidence on his clothing and the car pointed to his direct involvement. The motive for the crime also became clearer as investigators delved into the Andersons' financial situation. Jesse had taken out a substantial life insurance policy on Barbara shortly before her death, indicating a financial motive for the murder.

Faced with mounting evidence, Jesse was arrested and charged with first-degree intentional homicide. He pleaded not guilty, maintaining his story of the fictitious attackers.

Trial and Conviction

Jesse Anderson's trial began in August 1992, and it quickly became a media spectacle. The prosecution presented a compelling case, meticulously dismantling Jesse's fabricated narrative and presenting damning evidence against him. Witnesses testified about the couple's troubled marriage, Jesse's purchase of the knife and hat, and the forensic evidence that contradicted his story.

The defense attempted to cast doubt on the prosecution's case by questioning the handling of evidence and suggesting that the investigation had been flawed. However, the overwhelming evidence against Jesse made it difficult for the defense to sway the jury.

After a relatively short deliberation, the jury found Jesse Anderson guilty of first-degree intentional homicide. He was sentenced to life in prison without the possibility of parole, a sentence that reflected the brutal nature of the crime and the premeditation involved.

Imprisonment and Death

Jesse Anderson was sent to the Columbia Correctional Institution in Portage, Wisconsin, to serve his life sentence. His notoriety made him a target within the prison, and he struggled to adapt to life behind bars.

On November 28, 1994, Jesse Anderson was attacked by fellow inmates Christopher Scarver and another inmate, who was later identified as Joseph Paul Franklin, a white supremacist serial killer. The attack occurred in the prison's gymnasium, where Scarver and Franklin used a metal bar to bludgeon Anderson and fellow inmate Jeffrey Dahmer, the infamous serial killer. Anderson and Dahmer both succumbed to their injuries shortly after the attack.

Scarver later stated that he had been provoked by both Anderson and Dahmer and felt a sense of divine justice in carrying out the attacks. The murders of Anderson and Dahmer within the prison walls raised significant concerns about inmate safety and the management of high-profile prisoners.

Aftermath and Reflections

The murder of Barbara Anderson and the subsequent trial and conviction of Jesse Anderson had far-reaching implications. The case highlighted issues related to domestic violence, racial manipulation, and the complexities of the criminal justice system. It also underscored the tragic consequences of unchecked control and manipulation within a marriage.

Barbara's family and friends were left to grapple with their grief and the loss of a beloved wife and mother. The community of Cedarburg was similarly shaken by the crime, as it shattered the veneer of a peaceful suburban life. The case remains a cautionary tale about the dangers of domestic violence and the need for vigilance and support for those in abusive relationships.

Legacy and Lessons Learned

The legacy of Jesse Anderson's crime is multifaceted. It serves as a stark reminder of the devastating impact of domestic violence and the importance of addressing and intervening in such situations before they escalate to fatal outcomes. The case also highlighted the pernicious effects of racial manipulation and the exploitation of societal prejudices for personal gain.

In the years since the crime, there have been ongoing efforts to improve support systems for victims of domestic violence and to raise awareness about the signs and dangers of abusive relationships. The case has also been studied in criminal justice and psychology circles as an example of the lengths to which individuals may go to cover up their crimes and manipulate public perception.

Barbara Anderson's memory lives on through her family and the community that mourned her loss. Her tragic death continues to inspire efforts to combat domestic violence and support those in need. The case of Jesse Anderson, meanwhile, serves as a grim reminder of the consequences of unchecked control, manipulation, and violence within intimate relationships.

Conclusion

The story of Jesse Anderson and the murder of Barbara Anderson is a dark chapter in Wisconsin's history. It is a tale of manipulation, control, and the devastating impact of domestic violence. The crime, trial, and subsequent events surrounding Jesse Anderson's life and death provide a sobering reflection on the complexities of human behavior and the importance of justice and support for victims of violence.

As we remember Barbara Anderson and the tragic events that unfolded in 1992, it is crucial to continue working towards a society where such acts of violence are prevented, and where victims are supported and protected. The lessons learned from this case must not be forgotten, and the efforts to combat domestic violence and promote justice must remain steadfast.

Jesse Anderson

Final Thoughts

Final Thoughts on "Blood in the Heartland: Notorious Wisconsin Murders"

"Blood in the Heartland: Notorious Wisconsin Murders" delves into some of the darkest and most disturbing crimes that have plagued the state of Wisconsin. As the author of this book, reflecting on the content and impact of the stories shared within its pages brings both a sense of gravity and profound realization. This book has explored the shadowy corners of Wisconsin's history, unveiling cases that range from the heinous to the perplexing, and it stands as a testament to the complexity of human nature and the dark undercurrents of American life.

The Essence of Darkness and Human Nature

At the core of "Blood in the Heartland" lies a profound exploration of human nature's darkest aspects. Each case documented within the book is a grim reminder of the capacity for violence that exists within individuals and the often-incomprehensible motives behind such acts. The murders discussed are not merely isolated incidents; they reflect broader societal issues, including mental health struggles, socioeconomic factors, and the influence of personal and familial dysfunction.

The nature of these crimes—whether driven by greed, passion, or sheer malice—illustrates the myriad ways in which human motivations can lead to acts of unspeakable violence. Understanding these cases requires delving into the psychology of the perpetrators, examining their backgrounds, and exploring the circumstances that led to their horrific actions. By analyzing these elements, the book seeks to provide a nuanced perspective on why individuals commit such atrocities and what societal factors may contribute to such behavior.

The Role of Media and Public Perception

The cases highlighted in "Blood in the Heartland" have not only impacted the victims and their families but also shaped public perception and media narratives. The sensationalism that often accompanies high-profile murders can skew public understanding and overshadow the complexities of each case. This book aims to cut through the media frenzy and offer a more grounded and factual account of these notorious murders.

Media coverage plays a significant role in shaping the public's perception of crimes and criminals. The way these stories are presented can influence everything from public opinion to judicial outcomes. For instance, the portrayal of suspects and victims in the media often affects how justice is perceived and administered. By presenting these cases with a focus on factual accuracy and context, "Blood in the Heartland" seeks to provide a balanced view that respects the gravity of the crimes while avoiding the pitfalls of sensationalism.

The Impact on Victims and Communities

The murders discussed in this book have left indelible marks on the victims and their communities. Each case represents not just a criminal act but a profound loss for families and a disruption to the social fabric of the affected communities. The emotional and psychological impact on the victims' families is immeasurable, and the long-term effects of such tragedies extend far beyond the immediate aftermath.

In recounting these stories, it is crucial to remember and honor the victims, acknowledging their humanity and the profound sorrow experienced by their loved ones. The book strives to respect their memories and the pain endured by those left behind. It also highlights the resilience of communities that have been scarred by violence but have come together to seek justice and support one another through the healing process.

Legal and Societal Implications

The notorious murders explored in this book also have significant legal and societal implications. Each case has prompted discussions about the effectiveness of the criminal justice system, the challenges of law enforcement, and the need for reforms. Issues such as the adequacy of forensic techniques, the handling of evidence, and the treatment of suspects and witnesses are central to these discussions.

Furthermore, these cases underscore the importance of addressing underlying social issues that contribute to criminal behavior. Efforts to improve mental health services, address socioeconomic disparities, and enhance community support systems are crucial in preventing future tragedies. By examining these cases, "Blood in the Heartland" contributes to ongoing conversations about how to build safer and more just societies.

Reflection on the Writing Process

Writing "Blood in the Heartland: Notorious Wisconsin Murders" has been a journey of deep reflection and emotional engagement. Delving into the details of such grim stories requires a careful balance between sensitivity and objectivity. The goal has been to present these cases with the respect they deserve while providing an insightful analysis of the factors involved.

The writing process has involved extensive research, including reviewing court documents, interviewing experts, and consulting various sources to ensure accuracy and depth. It has also required grappling with the emotional weight of the subject matter and maintaining a focus on the broader implications of the stories told.

Final Reflections on the Book's Contribution

As we close the final chapter of "Blood in the Heartland," it is important to reflect on the book's contribution to understanding the darker side of Wisconsin's history. The goal has been to offer a comprehensive and thought-provoking examination of notorious murders, shedding light on the complexities of criminal behavior, the impact on victims and communities, and the broader societal issues at play.

The stories within this book are a stark reminder of the challenges faced by individuals and communities in confronting violence and seeking justice. They serve as a call to action for continued efforts to address the root causes of criminal behavior and to support those affected by violence. By exploring these cases with sensitivity and rigor, "Blood in the Heartland" contributes to a deeper understanding of the human condition and the ongoing quest for justice.

Moving Forward: Lessons Learned

The lessons learned from examining these notorious Wisconsin murders extend beyond the specific cases discussed. They highlight the need for ongoing vigilance in addressing the factors that contribute to criminal behavior, the importance of supporting victims and their families, and the necessity of ensuring that justice is served fairly and effectively.

In moving forward, it is essential to continue exploring the complex issues related to crime and justice, to support efforts aimed at preventing violence, and to advocate for reforms that enhance the effectiveness and fairness of the criminal justice system. The stories told in "Blood in the Heartland" remind us of the ongoing need for compassion, understanding, and commitment to creating safer and more equitable communities.

Concluding Thoughts

"Blood in the Heartland: Notorious Wisconsin Murders" is more than a collection of true crime stories; it is a reflection on the darker aspects of human nature and the societal issues that contribute to criminal behavior. The book aims to provide a comprehensive and nuanced understanding of notorious murders in Wisconsin, shedding light on the complexities of these cases and their broader implications.

As we conclude this exploration, it is important to remember that the stories told within these pages represent real lives and real tragedies. The book seeks to honor the memory of the victims, respect the struggles of their families, and contribute to ongoing discussions about justice and prevention. Through this journey into the heart of darkness, "Blood in the Heartland" invites readers to reflect on the challenges and opportunities for creating a more just and compassionate society.

ABOUT THE AUTHOR

 Scott E. Bowser is the author of four non-fiction books, Gein (2021), The Travelers Guide to Ed Gein (2021) and The Ed Gein Chronicles (2023) Wisconsin Ghostly Legends (2024). Scott appeared on MGM Plus tv show "Psyco: The Lost Tapes of Ed Gein".

Scott was born in 1964, in Kingsford, Michigan and lived his young years in Neenah, Wisconsin. Scott always had an interest in true crime and the paranormal whether it be reading about it or watching it on tv.

Scott now lives in Wisconsin Rapids. Wisconsin where in his spare time he gives Ed Gein tours in Plainfield, Wisconsin. Scott also in his spare time creates children and adult coloring books which all are also available on Amazon. He is currently writing a screenplay for his first book "Gein".

Other Books by Scott Bowser

Available on Amazon and at Barnes & Noble

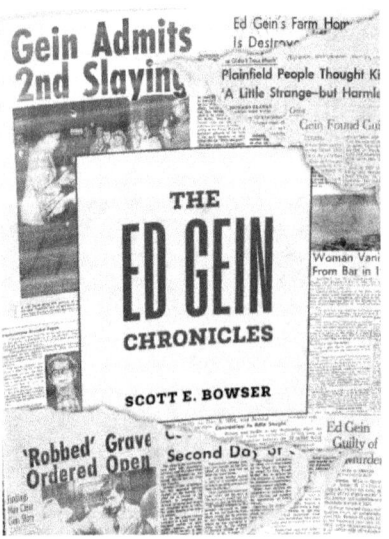 

www.ingramcontent.com/pod-product-compliance
Lightning Source LLC
LaVergne TN
LVHW012018060526
838201LV00061B/4365